# What's in Your CORE?

# What's in Your CORE?

## An Educator's Guide to Plugging into Purpose and Perspective

Gary Goelz and Greg Goelz

ROWMAN & LITTLEFIELD
*Lanham • Boulder • New York • London*

Published by Rowman & Littlefield
An imprint of The Rowman & Littlefield Publishing Group, Inc.
4501 Forbes Boulevard, Suite 200, Lanham, Maryland 20706
www.rowman.com

6 Tinworth Street, London SE11 5AL, United Kingdom

Copyright © 2020 by Gary Goelz and Greg Goelz

*All rights reserved.* No part of this book may be reproduced in any form or by any electronic or mechanical means, including information storage and retrieval systems, without written permission from the publisher, except by a reviewer who may quote passages in a review.

British Library Cataloguing in Publication Information Available

**Library of Congress Cataloging-in-Publication Data Available**

ISBN 978-1-4758-5686-6 (cloth : alk. paper)
ISBN 978-1-4758-5687-3 (pbk. : alk. paper)
ISBN 978-1-4758-5688-0 (electronic)

*This book is dedicated to my twin brother and coauthor, our incredibly supportive wives and amazing children, and is written with sincere gratitude to all of our fellow educators who keep kids at their core.*

# Contents

| | |
|---|---|
| Foreword | ix |
| **PART I: A FIRST BITE INTO THE CORES** | **1** |
| Twinning and Winning! | 3 |
| Introduction | 5 |
|   1  What's in Your CORE? | 11 |
| **PART II: PICKING AND CONSUMING THE TEN CORES** | **17** |
|   2  Advocate | 19 |
|   3  Changer | 33 |
|   4  Character-Builder | 51 |
|   5  Collaborator | 71 |
|   6  Connector | 89 |
|   7  Energizer | 109 |
|   8  Helper | 127 |
|   9  Innovator | 145 |
| 10  Leader | 161 |

| 11 | Preparer | 177 |

**PART III: YOU ATE TO THE APPLE CORE: NOW WHAT?** **195**

| 12 | Time for Apple Pie | 197 |

| Bibliography | 203 |
| About the Authors | 205 |

# Foreword

All educators have their own unique story that is their "why" they got into education. Additionally, all educators have their collection of "ah-ha" moments that they will always remember when they made a significant and lasting difference in the lives of those they teach or work with. It's the reason people get into education. For example, as a teacher and administrator, when I work with students or staff and there is one of those special moments, it creates a special feeling deep within me. It's hard to explain, but it's like a buzz that reverberates throughout my entire being. It is almost literally an electric feeling: an adrenaline rush. As an educator yourself, you know what I mean. Those are the moments that make the long hours, the daily frustrations and many challenges all worth it. However, if we're being honest, over time, those moments of joy can be replaced by the seemingly insurmountable stressors of any job in education.

As I write this, I realize it's ironic that I have never shared that perspective with anyone before, but I am now describing it to introduce this unique and amazing book, *What's In Your CORE?* That is the impact this book had on me. It prompted me to share something that is deep within me, at my core, but I had chosen not to share in my twenty-plus years in education. The book helped me to redefine my purpose for what I do. If you're looking for a way to deeply reflect (in a fun way) and rekindle your passion to create more "ah-ha" moments in your classroom or school, then you've picked the right book.

In *What's In Your CORE?*, educators will be able to define, articulate, and reframe discussions about passion, purpose, and perspective. Gary and Greg Goelz do not bore you by proposing new theory or sharing research studies that would make you feel like you have to add more "to-do" items to your list in order to be effective. Instead, the Goelz brothers offer you opportunities for reflection and immediate practical application, ways you can improve yourself and your service to others tomorrow. They want you to remember who you are as an educator and fully leverage your talents to benefit those around you. They will ask you to consider your own practice as well as give you insight and perspective on those who you work with.

*What's in Your CORE?* is unlike any educational book I've ever read. Gary and Greg create ten COREs (Callings Or Reasons in Education) that are basically educational personality types. The explanation of these COREs allows you to ponder which ones you most connect with in terms of your own purpose as an educator. And, perhaps more importantly, you'll consider the COREs of those you work with so that you can better understand their perspective. They masterfully intertwine professional and personal stories and quotes from both nationally known educators and educators like you, in classrooms today, to illustrate their points and to push the reader into deep introspection. The book provides great teachable moments, perspective-taking scenarios for discussion, reflective questions, and "I Dare You" prompts to elicit even more action. It is insightful, fun, and easy to read and gives any K-12 educator or leader an opportunity to grow professionally.

I know that as you read *What's In Your CORE?* it will remind you of why you got into education, give you better perspective of those you work with, and provide you with the necessary tools to create more "ah-ha" moments for your students and staff. I have no doubt that if you APPLeY (this concept will make sense as you read the book) what you have learned from Gary and Greg, you will become the best version of yourself, which will create more "buzz" moments for you, your students, and your fellow educators.

I believe that busy educators like you who care deeply about the students you serve will benefit greatly from reading this book. Quite frankly, it's worth your valuable time. I'm confident that you will not only rekindle your passion for the profession and better understand those around you, but will also use this book as a stepping stone for more student success than you could have previously imagined. Enjoy the book!

Paul Mielke, Ph.D.
Hamilton School District superintendent and author
of *Making Teachers Better Not Bitter*

*Part I*

# A FIRST BITE INTO THE CORES

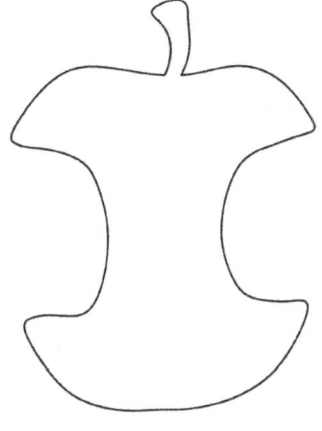

# Twinning and Winning!

Gary Goelz    Greg Goelz

Our Family: Mike, Marv, Cleone, Jeff and "The Twins"

*Greg:* Hey, twin brother, I was born three minutes before you. So I'll start, right?
*Gary:* Of course you will.
*Greg:* It's not my fault, it's mom's.
*Gary:* Yes, I'm used to that very logical reasoning by now.
*Greg:* Come on, give me a break here. Being born first was the last time I beat you at anything.
*Gary:* Oh brother (pun intended), here we go again.
*Greg:* Ok, here goes nothing.

We are fraternal twins, born in September of 1974. Our childhood growing up in a suburb just outside of Milwaukee, Wisconsin, could be considered the stuff of "Leave it to Beaver" or "Happy Days." Life was idyllic, easy, and fun. Our mother worked part time and did most of the "raising" of the children. Our father was the breadwinner who did "fatherly" things like "provide," drive us to and from various practices, and mow the lawn every Saturday morning. We have two older brothers (we'll call them Jeff and Mike, since those are their real names), who carefully balanced both caring for us and reminding us in subtle and not-so-subtle ways that we were their younger brothers and were to be kept in our place.

One brother in particular, Jeff, did so repeatedly and has therefore earned many references in personal stories that we share at the beginning of each chapter. You're welcome, Jeff. To be completely honest, an extra motivator to write this book was to keep the promise we made to Jeff that we would someday get revenge. Well Jeff, today is that day.

In high school, we swam competitively, shared many things including some of the same friends, and both graduated in 1992 (due to alphabetical order, Gary did so moments before Greg). We both went to college at the University of Wisconsin-Whitewater. Although neither of us initially intended on majoring in education, not many years later, that's exactly where we found ourselves. And, thank goodness! We graduated with our bachelor's degrees at the same time . . . well, again, Gary received his moments before Greg. (Come to think of it, Gary went on to earn his master's degree first too . . . dang it!)

Collectively, we've spent over forty years in education. Initially, Gary as an elementary teacher and Greg a school counselor. Later, Gary became a principal and an assistant superintendent, then decided to return to the elementary classroom to teach kids again. Greg has had various roles, mostly in school counseling and special education supervision, and currently serves as the principal of an alternative education high school which uses project-based learning principles.

*Greg:* So, we'll both take turns doing the writing?
*Gary:* Yes, taking turns just like mom and dad taught us to many years ago!
*Greg:* So how did I do so far?
*Gary:* Excellent.
*Greg:* Really?
*Gary:* Mom told me to say that.

# Introduction

**FOCUS ON THE APPLE, NOT THE TREE**

We believe in the power of education, and in every single educator across the nation. We believe in the incredible potential that every educator has to change kids' lives every day, regardless of role. We believe in you, our fellow educators. However, as they say these days, *"the struggle is real."*

We also believe that all too often school staff gradually (and sometimes not so gradually) lose their way from what got them into the profession. Away from the talents, excitement, drive, and skill set that drew them to the field in the first place. They lose their passion to not only *reach* students, but to *reach* them in a meaningful way. The passion to not only do the *work*, but to do the *work* in a meaningful way. A way that deeply impacts students today and forever.

Let's face it, education has reached a point where many talented, quality educators are leaving the profession. And, the truth is, there are fewer and fewer college students selecting education as their major and thus less applicants for teaching vacancies out in the "real world." We can come up with all kinds of reasons as to why we think that may be, but what it often comes down to is day-to-day **purpose and fulfillment**. There is a disconnect between what current teachers signed up for years ago and their current reality. That disconnect ranges from disappointing to downright unbearable. Reading this book will help you as an educator reconnect with what's in your core, why you got into education in the first place.

You've quite possibly heard of the saying *"being too close to the forest to see the (apple) trees,"* referring to not being able to see the big picture. But what if, as an educator in any role, you could step *even* closer and focus only on the apple? The apple quite literally is the fruit of the labor of the tree, the reason it exists. Instead of focusing on all of the "other" things that have been added to your plate beyond directly working with kids, what if you could remain focused on your reason for choosing the field of education in the first place? That is, each student, one at a time.

For a teacher, instead of looking at your class as a whole, which can at times feel overwhelming and stressful, look at the positive attributes each individual student brings. For a school leader, instead of looking at your staff as a whole (which also can feel overwhelming and stressful!), look at them as individuals and the amazing people and educators that they are. See them for their many strengths. See the apple, not the forest. In the meantime, while reading this book, we want you to reclaim and maximize what's at your core, the reason you do what you do.

## PURPOSE AND PERSPECTIVE

Most educators believe that they were "called" in some way to education. Of those educators, nearly all begin their career with an "I will change the world" mentality. Over time, however, the stressors of the job may pull them away from this feeling, away from the very reason or purpose they were called. They might even ponder at times if, years ago, becoming an educator was the right choice. Essentially, they may question if there is a true alignment between their calling for being in education with their daily work with students. They know that when there is alignment, there is also a sense of pride, of doing important work, of making an impact, and if we're being honest, a desire to get out of bed each morning and go do the important work. This impact is aligned with why they answered the call years ago. **The truth is,**

**most educators at some time lose sight of their purpose, and their perspective, about their role**.

This book is designed to help all educators get back to the CORE of what they love most about the profession (other than summer break, but let's be fair, right?). To affirm the very thing that brings them to, or perhaps back to, feeling satisfied, proud, and positive about their work with students. When we say "all" educators, we mean just that. Whether you're a teacher, an aide, a principal, a district office leader, or anyone in between, this book is for you.

Regardless of your role, we know you're a busy educator, looking to apply what you learn from any educational book. So, in addition to a very intentional structure of the book which naturally lends itself to practical application, we've also included several "APPLeY It!" sections throughout every CORE chapter. These sections offer practical ideas to take what you're learning about and implement them for your students immediately.

We believe that our varied K-12 experiences, in both urban and suburban settings, will help any educator connect with this book. In working with hundreds of people over the years, we've found that educators can always articulate *"what"* they do, but they sometimes stumble when we ask *"why"* they do it. We often get the "textbook" answers of *"I love children!"* or *"I want to help people!"* While these of course are true, it's important to go deeper. Do you really know and understand what led you to the profession? More importantly, do you remember the things we you find most satisfying about the job, the CORE of why you do what you do each day?

In this book, our two distinctive voices—both working in education—**explain a set of attributes that help educators affirm the "why."** In doing so, *"What's In Your CORE?"* renews the reason we believe in the future of schools and why we want you to reidentify, reclaim, and maximize your **purpose** as an educator. Then, we want you to gain a firm understanding of what your colleagues' COREs are **(perspective)** in order to team together to efficiently achieve goals.

## CORES AREN'T JUST FOR APPLES
## ... WHAT'S IN YOUR CORE?

We will introduce you to what we refer to as a person's **CORE (their Calling Or Reason in Education)**. There are ten COREs that we've created. Educators possess strength in one or several of them, but not all. Once identified, doing so helps you not only affirm and maximize your purpose, but also better understand the perspectives of your colleagues who may be strong in different areas. **Think of the COREs as your "educational personality type" or your default setting.**

Throughout the book, you will feel challenged to examine why you initially entered the field of education, any transformations you may have gone through along the way, and, ultimately, return to your main calling (*purpose*) for being an educator. This main "calling" or "reason" will then assist you, along with school leaders, to fully utilize those skills and talents to achieve individual and school goals. It will also allow you to better understand where your colleagues are coming from in given situations (*perspective-taking*). And, in doing so, the team will then better recognize, understand, and thrive on the positive attributes of each member.

We have considered dozens of potential "callings" or "reasons" and determined that there are ten main components (bites) we refer to as "COREs." Here they are, along with their definitions:

| COREs | |
|---|---|
| Advocate | Connector |
| Changer | Energizer |
| Character-Builder | Helper |
| Collaborator | Innovator |
| Leader | Preparer |

CORE Definitions:

1. Advocate—champions what is right by being a tireless voice for others
2. Changer—improves current systems by challenging the status quo
3. Character-Builder—moves beyond academics to focus on the whole child and creating better people
4. Collaborator—unifies and empowers others to achieve shared goals together
5. Connector—understands and is committed to the strength of relationships
6. Energizer—spreads their positive attitude, joy and fun in all they do

7. Helper—serves the needs of others before all else
8. Innovator—fearlessly creates and accomplishes the unimaginable
9. Leader—creates, supports, monitors, and facilitates the work
10. Preparer—connects learning to life in a way that gets students ready for their future

## NOW, STEP BACK TO SEE THE WHOLE ORCHARD

We believe that schools, like any business or organization, get very accustomed to operating in the same ways, year after year. Operating in ways that may be comfortable, but not necessarily right or efficient. Ways that silo people based on job title, rather than creating an explosion of progress by merging people and their talents together in the right places. We believe that people, over time, are the same way. Educators can get bogged down in the day-to-day of your jobs, losing touch with your own "way." But, what if there was a way to help all educators be reminded of, and reconnect with, your own personal "why." And, more importantly, a way to take advantage of what's in your CORE, not so much in your job description, to maximize your impact on an entire school or district.

Moving beyond reflecting on one's personal CORE, this same concept affords school leaders the ability to have a clearer picture of the strengths and motivations of every staff person they support. They can avoid the trap of assigning tasks based on job title, rather than actual strengths of individuals. This also accelerates the learning curve so school leaders can get to know their staffs quicker, in a more meaningful way, by getting to know their COREs. It saves time and resources when assigning staff to duties, committees, and class assignments. It helps not only get the right people on the bus, but also to get them in the right seats.

For example: Instead of every teacher in your school having the exact same out-of-classroom "duties" like before and after school student drop-off supervision (Energizer CORE), being grade or department representative at school leadership meetings (Leader CORE), and working on school schedules (Preparer CORE), what if there was another way? What if teachers who loved working on schedules but didn't love before and after school student drop-off duty, well, worked on schedules and didn't have any student drop-off duty? Because, well, other teachers are stronger in the Energizer CORE that is required for that duty and thus took an extra drop-off duty so they didn't have to support working on school schedules (which they dread more than, well, whatever it is that they dread)?

As fellow educators, we want to thrive, not just survive, every day in the difficult jobs that we have chosen. We want the same for you. Part of that is being reminded of why you got into the profession in the first place. Another part of that is reclaiming and maximizing that purpose. If you're interested in either, read on. If you're not, read on anyway! We promise that this book will be different from any other you've ever read.

*Chapter 1*

# What's in Your CORE?

**Ultimately, this book is about two things: Purpose and Perspective. Meaning: reclaiming and fully utilizing your own purpose in order to feel fulfilled . . . and . . . understanding and trusting the perspectives of those you work with to accomplish school goals.** More to come on these two themes as they are woven into the fabric of the book.

Moving on, we would like to offer an apology. We realize that books don't typically begin with an apology, but this book isn't like most books. The fact is, most people in education read a professional book to learn a new skill, philosophy, strategy, or program. This is due to our own quest to continuously improve and be the lifelong learners that we know we must be, to add "tools to our toolbox." Well, we're sorry (sort of), but **this book will not teach you to be someone or something that you're not already.**

It will not proclaim to have the newest, brightest, shiniest concept that, if you integrate into your practice, will make you a more impactful educator. After all, the pendulum tends to swing back and forth (and back and forth) on many of those shiniest "new" things anyways. Our book actually contradicts the notion that we should continue to pile on more and more of what's new, the next fads in education. Instead, this book is about returning to the mountain of good that is already there inside of you, at your CORE . . . that you have not yet realized. Or, more likely, over the years things that have fallen by the wayside due to "everything else" that as an educator you are charged to do every day. We get it, we're right there alongside you, doing the same work. **We are not going to tell you what or who you should be. We are going to help you remember who you already are, then how to fully leverage that.**

We'll help you return to your purpose. So, in all honesty, if you're reading this book to find out what "more" you should be doing for your students, put it down. Ok, don't actually put it down (we've got kids to put through college). But, change your perspective about what you are going to get out of it, or better yet about your approach to improving as an educator (not "more," rather "re-aligned with purpose").

This book will also offer a powerful challenge: to look deeply inside yourself and make some decisions that could impact the rest of your professional and personal life. Sounds a little uncomfortable and maybe a little scary, right? Well, good. This book will force you to take a clear look at yourself and who you've become as an educator. Then, you'll make crucial decisions as far as what to do next. Ask yourself the question, *"Is my role in education everything I thought it would be when I first signed up?"* If you're being completely honest, it's probably not. In fact, your true answer might be, well, a lot more "colorful" than that! It's ok. Being an educator is a tough job, one that seems to get more challenging as the years go by. However, it's also an awesome job, one where you truly make an impact on the world, one student at a time! That's where this book comes in. Are you ready? Do you accept the challenge?

## FOUNDATION (THE WHY)

You've likely heard the phrase, *"Begin with the end in mind."* which is the second habit from Stephen Covey's *"The 7 Habits of Highly Effective People."* What he teaches us, of course, is the importance of knowing where your final destination is, so that then, and only then, can you map out how to get there. If you think about this phrase more in terms of mapping out your professional life as an educator, you're thinking about the kind of educator you aspire to be by the end of your career, and then take steps to get there. If you're thinking about beginning with the end in mind when you're writing a book, you consider what you want the reader to get out of it by the end of the book, and plan backward from there.

So, before we dive into what quite literally is at the CORE of this book (see what we did there?), as fellow educators we want to begin with the "why." As authors of this book, we think it is important to do the same here.

*Why did we write this book?* We wrote it for you. We're in the field every day working for kids too. One of us is a teacher (the better-looking one), the other a building principal. We know what it's like to be in your shoes each day. However, instead of adding more to your plate (most days we feel like we need a platter anyway), we'd like to take some off. We want you to take a breath, take a step back and spend some time in the place where you truly remember why you chose education in the first place. We know you spend some days there, but wouldn't it be great to spend EVERY day in that place? It would be like going on an endless tropical vacation, where the white sandy beaches and sky blue water go on forever. (Ok, maybe not that great, but you get the point.) Maybe there's even a swim-up bar? We digress.

For some of you, this might mean the result is some minor tweaks to your way of thinking about your job moving forward. For others, you might be hitting the reset button. Either way is fine. We wrote this book for you.

## MORE ABOUT THE COREs

While we realize that you were introduced to the COREs earlier in the book, we thought it'd be beneficial to provide them to you again. Here they are:

| COREs | |
|---|---|
| Advocate | Connector |
| Changer | Energizer |
| Character-Builder | Helper |
| Collaborator | Innovator |
| Leader | Preparer |

We believe that certain COREs are innately in us, similar to personality traits. As we said earlier, **think of your CORE as your "educational personality type."** We want you to recognize, enhance, and capitalize on these attributes that are naturally inside of you. We believe that the act of intentionally identifying and leveraging the COREs within you will help you to enjoy your job more and better serve students. This will lead to personal fulfillment, higher student achievement, and school-wide goal attainment. Sounds awesome, right?

A main goal of this book is for you to learn about these COREs, reflect on and determine which ones live naturally inside of you, and consider how you can fully maximize them. Another goal of this book is to help you understand the perspectives of others who have strengths in different COREs and, in doing so, have a greater appreciation and trust for their role in educating kids. One final goal of the book is to make you laugh! While educating kids is a serious topic, we can have some fun while writing (and, more importantly, for you . . . reading) about it.

Notice that we have not talked about "teaching" you about how to "learn" to be a certain CORE. This book was not written for you to read through to pick a CORE that you want to be and then give you the script for how to become an educator who is strong in that CORE. This book will not provide you with the roadmap to become a certain CORE. We say, if you want to be that CORE and you're not it already, accept it. Sounds a little harsh, we know, but we'd rather you focus on your innate skills and talents than try to become something you're not. Said another way, an apple is an apple, don't try to make it an orange.

That's not to say that you won't learn about other COREs that you don't have as your own and pick up a few techniques for actions you could take to acquire some of those skills. You will. And, though that won't necessarily make you into someone who is naturally strong in that certain CORE, we hope in doing so you'll keep that learning front and center moving forward in your life, as well as gain perspective in your colleagues strong in that CORE.

For example, let's say that "Innovator" is not at your CORE. That's ok. But, the next time you are interacting with an Innovator in your school (that person who is always inventing new ways of doing things), not only will you be able to better accept their perspective but you may also better understand why they seem to be so comfortable taking risks and trying new things. That doesn't then make you someone especially strong in the Innovator CORE, but it will positively impact you and the kids you serve simply by understanding the Innovator's perspective. And, as we said, maybe you'll be more open yourself to innovating in the future.

Along with reading the book to assist you with identifying your CORE or COREs, it will also lead you to identifying the gaps in your own professional skill set. That's ok and actually a good thing! Sometimes identifying what we are not helps clarify what we are. Knowing our own limitations allows us to look for others who not only CAN fill the gaps but also WANT to fill the gaps and are fulfilled by it. **Stop trying to be an expert in everything and trying to do it all yourself and start trusting others to use their COREs for the common good.**

Now, as stated previously, we don't want you to skip the COREs that you don't identify with. On the contrary, read them just as close or closer than the CORE you believe is yours. A major part of this book is about perspective-taking; how both understanding the COREs of others and fully utilizing them lead to very powerful outcomes. When we are all "on the right seat on the bus" (for the purposes of this book, this means doing things for kids that align with our own CORE), very impactful things take place as far as results for students. And, well, um, you enjoy your job more. So, there's that.

Connected to that and, lastly, we promise you that **knowing and fully utilizing your CORE will lead to greater happiness and increased fulfillment in your job.** Remember feeling fulfilled in your job? Remember feeling energized when you used your CORE (whether you knew it or not) to reach a child or complete a difficult task? That CORE, that passion, that energy was there when you chose this profession. To some extent, it may have been covered up since then with layer after layer of other "stuff." But it IS still there! Let's uncover it together and get back to where you started.

## STRUCTURE OF CHAPTERS

In this book, each of the ten COREs (Calling Or Reason in Education) are given their own chapter. Each chapter is broken down in the following way:

1. Quote related to the CORE
2. Personal picture and story related to the CORE
3. Definition of the CORE
4. Research that supports the CORE and our interpretation of it
5. Real-world professional stories
6. Summary of the chapter
7. Perspective-Taking Scenario
8. Reflective questions (perspective and school outcomes based)
9. "We Dare You Challenge" statement
10. Now What?/Action Steps

We've been very intentional about this structure. We believe that each component is critical. Whether light and humorous or content-focused and grounded in research, each component will help the reader gain understanding and perspective about the COREs.

So, in conclusion, why read this book? No, seriously. You're a busy educator. We believe that the power from reading the book comes when staff members know and maximize their own individual attributes (their CORE), and also have the ability to gain a new perspective on how relying on each other's COREs leads to powerful outcomes for students. So, grab a colleague (and an apple) if you care to, and read on! Enjoy the first CORE!

*Part II*

# PICKING AND CONSUMING THE TEN CORES

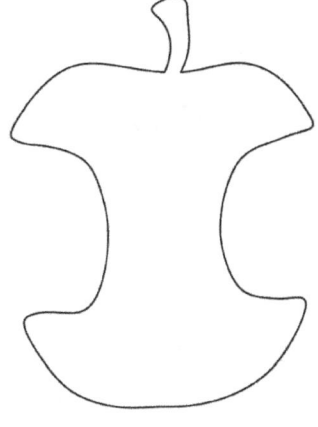

*Chapter 2*

# Advocate

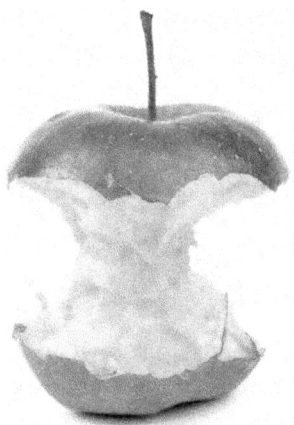

**Advocate**: champions what is right by being a tireless voice for others

*Every child deserves a champion—an adult who will never give up on them, who understands the power of connection and insists that they become the best that they can possibly be.*

—Rita Pierson

**Note for the reader:** Throughout this book, at the beginning of each chapter, we will include pictures of us growing up as they connect to a particular CORE. For your reading pleasure, really just to offer a laugh at our own expense, we'll also include a (hopefully humorous) caption further explaining the picture. Additionally, we'll include a personal story from our childhood. We hope that you find these additional pieces of our book unique, informational, and entertaining. Here are the first ones for the Advocate CORE.

**"Pssssst . . . Corduroy bibs?
And these hats? What was mom thinking?
I told you, we should have said something!"**

## PERSONAL STORY

Here's a personal story of when Greg needed an Advocate.

We were barely sixteen and just starting to drive. Our dad took us to a local high school parking lot on the weekends to teach us how. We drove a boxy, 4-door, silver, 1987 Toyota Corolla that neither of us will ever forget. Our dad (we'll call him Marv, mostly because that's his real name) loved that car. He washed and waxed it every weekend by hand (not really, but you get the point). We could have cared less. We just wanted to get our licenses so we could begin living life like a sixteen-year-old believes life should be.

We'd go to the parking lot together to practice, our dad in the passenger seat barking commands and the other one of us sitting in the backseat snickering, doing whatever we could to make the other brother make a mistake. Well, we both got our licenses (it took Gary two tries, for the record, at least that's how I like to remember it). But, Gary was the "golden child" of the family, so he seemed to get the use of the car a little more often than I did. More on the "golden child" piece as this story (and so many others) unfolds.

One night when he had the car, Gary returned home acting upset. He dramatically entered our kitchen from the garage to announce that he had hit a patch of ice on his way home and crashed the car. His alligator tears were in full effect and my twin senses were just as fully activated. I knew something was awry, but wasn't sure what. Gary went on to tell his tale of driving through a church parking lot as he came home from his girlfriend's house (the parking lot was a shortcut to get to the street that she lived on) when he "hit a patch of ice" and struck a light pole on the driver's side door. My father, without asking if he was alright, darted out to the car to find the driver's side door and frame badly damaged. As he was assessing the damage, my mother assessed any damage to Gary. No, he wasn't injured, but he was busy working his story. Our eyes met and he saw that I knew something was not adding up.

I started pouring on the questions, challenging him left and right as to exactly how this happened. His order of events seemed off. Why was there a delay in his coming home? Why didn't he call when this happened? Did this really happen on his way home? Or, did it happen hours ago and he then used the time to concoct this story? Why did he seem nervous? Why is he sweating profusely on a frigid, ten-degree night? So many questions. And, no answers . . . yet. This "golden child" was going down. Big time.

My father then returned from the garage and was taking in my questioning. He was really listening to Gary's answers. Would he finally be on my side for something? Did I catch the "do no wrong" brother in a lie? I was elated to be so close to finally taking him down a notch in my parents' eyes. Just then, and it happened quickly, my father's gaze drew to me. No! I thought. Look back at Gary! He is the one who is in trouble here! My father started asking me questions:

*Dad:* Where were YOU when this happened?
*Me:* I was home. For crying out loud, I was here with you! I was home!
*Dad:* Do YOU also drive carelessly in ice and snow?
*Me:* Well, yes, but I haven't been caught doing it or certainly haven't crashed the family car.
*Dad:* Did YOU model or in some way dare Gary to drive recklessly that led to this?
*Me:* No! What is happening here!

Well, what was happening was that somehow Gary had turned things around and I got partially, no mostly, blamed for crashing a car that I wasn't even in. This really happened. I believe the statement our father made was, "Well, even if you didn't do it this time, it's still something you would've done." And then he said something like, "If this could happen to Gary, I hope YOU learn a lesson from this." Over my father's right shoulder, Gary stood with a smirk. He had done it again, a master of deception and deflection. Right when I needed an advocate to champion what was right, when I needed my own twin brother to stand up for me and take the blame for the car he crashed, he wasn't there. Nice, real nice.

What really happened on that cold, blustery night in Wisconsin? Gary had been speeding around that church parking lot by his girlfriend's house doing figure eights around the light poles. He did indeed hit a patch of ice and hit a light pole, but it was no random accident. The final result of that night was that I was sent to my room without dinner. And Gary? I'm pretty sure he ate my dessert.

## ADVOCATE DEFINED

In regards to a CORE, we define an ADVOCATE as "champions what is right by being a tireless voice for others." Advocates, although not necessarily outwardly confident or assertive in their own personal lives, become both of these traits when speaking up for others. They take risks by speaking out when others won't. **Advocates place the needs of others first and are passionate about being the voice of the voiceless.** They support others, but aim to teach and empower so those they represent can move forward on their own. Advocates do not give up. Ever.

They don't look at roadblocks as barriers, rather, as challenges to break down what is wrong or perhaps confront the status quo. Lastly, advocates can appear at first to be a divisive force, but can actually have the opposite effect. Their challenges often reveal what is real, leading to clarification of the issue being discussed and, thus, more sound decisions. Advocates, when given a seat at the table and trusted, can be a unifying force.

We believe that the CORE of Advocate can best be further defined by breaking our definition down into four main subcategories as outlined below:

- A Voice for Those Without One
- A Tireless Defender of What Is Right
- Connects People to Needed Resources
- Provides a Different Way To Look At An Issue

As we further explain these subcategories, we'll include both supporting research and stories from ourselves and colleagues who have shared their experiences in education with us. Enjoy!

## A VOICE FOR THOSE WITHOUT ONE

Hopefully, we've all had someone in our lives who has spoken up for us when we most needed it. Besides a parent, for many of us it could be a coach, neighbor, teacher, aunt/uncle, family friend, or church leader (but likely not a twin brother who crashed a car). Whomever it was, we remember them for stepping in when we needed them. **The advocate is the person who swoops in and gives a renewed sense of hope.** And, when you think about those feelings that you have when you are on the receiving end of an advocate's gifts, it's a wonder why there aren't more advocates in the world. I mean, why wouldn't any of us want to provide that level of hope and inspiration?

We submit that every educator has the innate desire and ability to advocate for kids. The difference between any educator as compared to an educator who is an Advocate CORE is the frequency and degree (the "what") of their advocacy. Ridnouer states that a teacher as an advocate is "a person who supports or promotes the interests of another, and that is what a teacher is doing when he or she works to engage students and their parents as partners in a positive, learning-focused classroom community"(2011).

The power of this statement involves advocacy that reaches beyond the classroom. There is real power, of course, when a teacher advocates for the students in their class. However, when staff see their role as an advocate as one that extends beyond the class to the whole grade, school, district, or community, that's when the magic happens (perhaps not pulling a bunny out of a hat magic, but magic nonetheless).

> When I think about my purpose for being an educator, I think about making an impact. I want to impact students lives in a positive way so that hopefully someday they'll think back and remember how much I cared. Every student needs an advocate and someone who deeply cares about their well-being. (Laura, middle school teacher)

**An advocate naturally knows what is right and is comfortable making it known.** These opportunities to advocate may occur in very public places like staff meetings, parent/teacher conferences, parent council meetings, or school board meetings. They can also happen behind the scenes in more private settings including in a classroom with one teacher and his/her students. An advocate is the third grade teacher who covertly switches up student groups to include a quiet student with other students who they believe will encourage that student to speak up. An advocate is a lunchroom supervisor who connects a new student with people to sit with. An advocate is the special education case manager who speaks up for a student's needs in a meeting. What have you done lately to advocate for another?

> Educator: You're in the staff lunchroom and a teacher is venting about a student's behavior in their classroom. Instead of half-nodding in some sort of weird semi-agreement, ask about the students strengths, encouraging the teacher to build from there. Or share your own positive experiences with the student. If they could, the student would thank you.
>
> Leader: Your superintendent doesn't need another bobblehead. If he/she is planning an initiative that you're very confident won't go well at the school level when implementing for kids, respectfully say so, along with sharing an alternative action that you believe will get the results they're looking for. Uncomfortable? Yes. Advocate? For sure.

In a previous role as an elementary school principal, I had many opportunities to be an advocate. One year there was a second grade student whose parents were working through getting a divorce. With that came shared custody of their son. The advocacy piece for the student came into play when his mother made a comment to me about her belief that there was some verbal and physical abuse occurring at his father's home. She described the alleged physical abuse, which included his father pulling her son by the arm and pushing him. However, her son didn't want to talk about it. She claimed she had seen bruises after her son spent time with his dad. I took the appropriate next steps, including calling the school social worker for her expertise and leadership.

Advocacy for the student was needed as I determined that no one was being the voice for the child. Unfortunately, this happens regularly in schools. We focus on the problem and solving it, rather than slowing down and listening to the student. I'm sure we have all had moments where a student sits quietly idle as adults take over to "solve" a problem, only to have the student say a few words that provides the clarity that then directs the rest of the conversation and eventual solution.

In the case of this particular story, the school social worker and I prepared for a conversation with the boy, with the main goal of making sure that he left feeling like he had someone who he could trust and talk to. Although the relationship between his mother and father continued to be sensitive and volatile, giving this student a voice in a very difficult situation where he was torn between two parents was critical. But, more importantly, it took the needed steps towards improving his sense of trust, safety, and well-being. He knew he had a voice who would speak for him. He had an advocate.

## A TIRELESS DEFENDER OF WHAT IS RIGHT

One of the key elements to being an advocate is being relentless about defending what is right for someone else at all costs. (Think Luke Skywalker, Mr. Miyagi, or Indiana Jones.) Or, if these all sound unfamiliar to you, then you didn't grow up in the 1980s. Congratulations, you're younger than the authors of this book! (You also missed out on quite a few great movies.) This doesn't mean that the person fights every battle they see. It just means that when they lock in on something that isn't right, they will stay with it until it is resolved despite any challenges along the way.

**Advocates are focused, consistent and unrelenting**. They may even be the person at a staff meeting who talks and is immediately met with thoughts by some of their peers of, "Oh no, here we go again." It's important to keep that perspective when the advocate speaks up. Remember, they are doing so to make something better for someone else. Again, advocates won't typically back down. And, thank goodness they don't.

Galford puts it this way, "Advocates instinctively act as a spokesperson in a group. They tend to be articulate, rational, logical and persuasive. They also tend to be relentless, championing ideas or strategic positions"(2017). Using a sports analogy, advocates are people you definitely want on your team, but who you never want to face on the opposition. They could initially be perceived as pushy, but look closer. Advocates are simply very focused on the goal of advocating for what is right. They are resilient. They can overcome nearly any barrier put in their way.

Educator: The next time you have the feeling that you should speak up about something, but in the past would have sat in silence, don't hesitate. Be confident and speak your mind. Advocate.

Leader: Even if you don't agree with a staff person who comments against the group by offering an alternate opinion or viewpoint on a topic, publicly recognize the strength it took to take a stand. Doing so will build confidence in others to be an advocate for what they believe in.

In one school I worked in, staff meeting agendas were often derailed by tenured teachers who truly believed that "those students" attending from outside of our district were the problem students in our school. "They" were the ones being disrespectful to teachers, getting in fights, possessing drugs, bringing down test scores, and in general being "the problem." These unproductive, negative, and frankly inappropriate comments were allowed for a few weeks until an assistant principal noticed that these feelings were already embedded in other staff and students.

As he examined further, it was clear that this was also a community-wide perception, extending far beyond the walls of our school. He noticed that there were growing parent complaints about "those" students damaging the school's reputation and its reputation in the surrounding community.

And just who were "those" students? They were mostly underprivileged, underserved, undersupported, poor, minority students from single-parent households from the inner city of the large city that bordered our district. They were in our school through the open enrollment program. This assistant principal decided to take it a step further and review school data to determine if these perceptions were indeed true. He analyzed behavior data, test scores, grade point averages, failure rates, police citations, and postsecondary plans. He then cross-checked these with where students lived. His list revealed one critical finding. Do you know what it was?

In every area that he pulled data from, it revealed that nonresident students represented an almost exact proportional responsibility for the outcomes he had examined. So, if 11 percent of the school population was made up of nonresident students, they were found to be connected to about 11 percent of the behavioral referrals, fights, drug possessions, citations, and so on.

What had actually happened is that the city and school district demographics had changed. The school, as well as the community, needed to accept the changes going on in their neighborhoods and embrace the diversity that had begun to take place. His advocacy of the students attending on open enrollment changed perspectives of many educators and community members over time.

In this case, the assistant principal courageously brought his findings to the school staff (that had to be a fun drive in to work that morning, knowing he was going to upset some people by simply stating the facts). Essentially, he was simply the advocate for "those students." And "those teachers" struggled to comprehend what he was saying. Questions arose and he held his ground and calmly relayed the facts. Good, solid, reliable data, after all, is hard to argue.

It took time, but the school shifted most of its large staff to understand and embrace their students' diverse backgrounds. Training sessions were conducted on teaching strategies to meet the needs of every learner, ways to deal with trauma, equity, effects of poverty, and others. All because that lone assistant principal decided to not only investigate something that didn't sound right to him but also take the step of advocating for what was right.

It reminds me of a quote by Albert Einstein that I've always liked: "What is right is not always popular and what is popular is not always right."

## CONNECTS PEOPLE TO NEEDED RESOURCES

An advocate may not have all of the answers, but they know how to find the people who do. **Advocates** (similar to "Helpers," as described in another chapter) **are skilled at getting to the need and are resourceful to find ways to help.** They are constantly searching for new resources both within the school or district and around the community. School staff are expected to recognize environmental factors that affect learning and react to them. This is why we've dedicated an entire chapter of this book to being an advocate, so that you can better recognize these factors and be a champion for another.

Working with, and for, the whole child is the key. Most teachers are amazing these days at identifying barriers to students' learning that go beyond their intellectual abilities and potential. They understand the link with home and academic performance, divorce and level of focus, trauma and engagement, drug use and motivation, and so on. Norton, Kelly, and Battle recognize this link by stating, "Efforts to ameliorate or resolve the problems of children and youth that inhibit them from pursuing educational opportunities can prevent dropouts and mitigate behavioral problems" (2013). The more we as educators can connect the outside of school factors with inside of school performance, the better we can serve our students, families, and communities.

Educator: Don't ever allow yourself or your colleagues to make any educational plan or decision, for any student, without first knowing their *whole* story. No matter what. The student is depending on you.

Leader: Stop yourself if/when you realize that when you review data, you see numbers, not students. Drill down to data by student name and meet them if possible. *How can you effectively advocate for them if you've never even had a conversation?*

One of my first "real jobs" out of college was as a state-certified social worker. I worked in the city's child welfare system as a case manager where abuse and neglect rates were high, and worker turnover rates were even higher. My particular caseload had four different case managers in the last year, each one of them burning out quicker than the previous one. I took over a caseload where I was responsible for eighteen active cases with around fifty kids. All of the kids had been removed from their homes and I was to manage their out-of-home placements, mostly in foster homes. This included securing their placements, supporting their foster parents, providing for clothing allowances, supervising parental visits, preparing legal documents, attending court hearings, monitoring school performance, and referring for needed services.

Jaquan was one of my kids. When I met him, he was sixteen years old and living with a distant relative on the city's north side. He was reserved and untrusting. He spoke very quietly, and although typically clean, he wore the same clothes every time I saw him. He always had a backpack and no matter where I met with him, he always positioned himself near the door. Like any of the young people I was assigned to, I read Jaquan's file before I met him. Most of the fifty-plus kids I was assigned to had horrific stories that followed them to their out-of-home placements. The allegations made on their parents were often appalling. Jaquan's story was no different.

Jaquan had been removed from the care of his mother after he had been badly beaten up at his own house by his cousin. My two years with Jaquan (he turned eighteen and aged out of the system) involved tremendous advocacy. He was a sixteen-year-old in the foster care system, which as such meant he was pretty much unadoptable. He drifted from foster home to foster home because he would become angry and violent and have to leave. It took time for me to learn the systems in place and available for Jaquan, but I learned and built resources for him and other kids I worked with. He needed services for mental health, independent living, tutoring, mentoring, medical care, legal representation, employability skills, and learning to drive (not surprisingly, I took him to learn in an empty high school parking lot . . . and I didn't slide on ice into any light poles).

In schools, we often think of pupil services and special education personnel as natural advocates. We agree, but suggest that we all look closer as other advocates may be serving in what we may consider nontraditional roles. Are you one of them? We think so.

Educator: When an Advocate speaks against your "side" of an argument, trust that they believe in their perspective as much as you believe in yours. It's not about being right or wrong, it's about trusting their different viewpoint on a given situation.

Leader: Allow yourself to be vulnerable enough to back off your stance on a sensitive student issue when the student's advocate speaks on their behalf. Perhaps they're not enabling the student as you may originally think, but rather they're educating you.

## PROVIDES A DIFFERENT WAY TO LOOK AT AN ISSUE

This section is all about *perspective*; the different perspectives that advocates provide to school teams. Aside from providing a powerful voice for others, as mentioned previously, revealing different perspectives may be the most beneficial part of being an advocate. They're the people who say something and you think, *"Hmmm, I've never thought of it that way before."*

In schools we sometimes get so caught up in the conveyor belt of student problems that we think we've seen it all. We lump kids with similar backgrounds, achievement scores, home lives, and so on together. What worked for the last dozen kids in that similar situation will most certainly work for this one, right? Wrong. Advocates speak up in these situations for these kids. The kids that remind us that every single student and every single situation is different. And, we need to treat every one of these students and every single one of these situations with respect and care. Advocates more naturally know that than others. They can look at each student situation and provide a unique perspective, one that others cannot.

In the school setting, have the courage to accept the perspective of the advocate. Use it to maximize the services the school team agrees to provide. You don't necessarily have to agree with them, but allow yourself to consider their perspective. Even if you don't agree, you'll be in a better place having paused to do so.

> I believe that family and student outcomes can improve with the right support and that families need voice, choice, and access to make improvements in the quality of life. I know that when families' lives improve, their children do better in school. (CM, elementary teacher)

## SUMMARY

We define an Advocate as a person who "champions what is right by being a tireless voice for others." In this chapter, we have used both pertinent research and our stories to further explain and expand on this definition. We divided the definition into four sections. We believe that an advocate is: A Voice for Those Without One, A Tireless Defender of What Is Right, Connects People to Needed Resources, and Provides a Different Way To Look At An Issue.

Additionally, we'd like to highlight a few specific components of the chapter that we believe are most important. We hope these are "take-aways" for you, little tidbits of information that will change you in your role in education:

- *"Dad, it was me who crashed the car. I was driving recklessly on the ice. Greg had nothing to do with it. I feel like I must speak up for him."* (Note that this has never been and will never actually be said . . . ever.)
- Advocates can appear at first to be a divisive force, but can actually have the opposite effect. Their challenges often **reveal what is real**, leading to clarification of the issue being discussed and, thus, more focused and sound decisions. Advocates, when given a seat at the table and trusted, can be a unifying force for schools staffs.
- A true advocate **uses their voice for others**, not for themselves. Think about it.

- **YOU are an Advocate**, regardless of your role in education. Who needs your voice today?

In this first CORE chapter, we also discussed two other salient points that are worth briefly revisiting. The first is purpose. You learned about the purpose and importance of Advocates in your school. You learned what Advocates specifically do, and why they are important to have in the school where you serve. The second is perspective. We hope that you've gained perspective about the Advocate, especially if perhaps your talents and skills don't align with having Advocate as one of your COREs. After reading this chapter, you now have a perspective about where they're coming from.

While we will weave in purpose and perspective throughout the book, we urge you to keep them front and center in your mind as you read on.

## Perspective-Taking Scenario

You are a fourth grade teacher in an upper-middle-class, suburban elementary school where most students come from supportive, two-parent households that are very involved in their children's education. You are at a student support meeting for a child from your classroom who is struggling. The team members present are prepared to develop a school plan to increase academic outcomes for this student who is struggling academically due to what has been deemed to be a lack of motivation. You are present as the classroom teacher and quickly realize that although the intention is good, the school team doesn't know the student very well and is developing a plan based strictly on test scores, behavioral data, and past practices that worked with other students. The team is focused on a plan that includes mostly punitive responses like being kept in at recess, talked to by administrator, parent contacts, and so on.

As the classroom teacher, you know the family story, which is that the child is currently living with his single mom who is struggling with drug addiction. The child stays with his aunt when his mother is gone during long bouts of sustained drug use. The aunt lives in a small apartment with her four children and her boyfriend. Your student sleeps on the couch and often comes to school tired, hungry, and distant. You know the student needs breakfast each morning, a trusted person to talk to, and a designated discreet spot to go should he need a break from the constant stress that is his life. Your belief is that the supports being offered at this meeting will not have the desired impact because they are mainly reactive in nature and fail to consider the environmental factors this student is struggling with. What do you say as far as offering proactive action steps so that you can act as the "champion" or "tireless voice" for your student?

## CORE Questions to Consider

1. Reflect on when someone has advocated for you. Where would you be had they not?
2. How will you integrate this learning about being an advocate into your daily practice?
3. How does a school fully leverage staff members who are strong in this CORE to lead to better school outcomes?

## We Dare You Challenge

Think of the most challenging (and perhaps frustrating) student you currently work with. I dare you to stick up for them the next time a colleague who also works with that student complains about them. Be respectful yet firm. You've succeeded if you can shift the conversation from complaining, to supporting and problem-solving. Then, take an action step, based on the conversation, to be an advocate for that student.

## Now What?/Action Steps

If this is your CORE, you should use it for the following actions:

- Constantly and confidently give a different perspective
- Provide a voice for those without one
- Speak up FOR things that are happening, not just AGAINST them but others also
- Refer students/families to resources that fulfill their needs

Why Every Team Needs Someone with the Advocate CORE

- To stand up for what is right for kids
- To respectfully challenge the way it's always been done
- To make sure everyone's thoughts/perspectives are equally represented
- To create/enhance a collaborative environment where all ideas are heard and valued
- To teach other team members to find their advocacy voice (power of modeling)

How Identifying People with the Advocate CORE Helps My School Leader

- They have a "go-to" person when they need someone with this skill set
- They can access this person when they are out of their comfort zone with an issue/concern
- Helps balance committees/teams
- Leads to sound decisions since all voices are heard
- Increases sense of school community

How Understanding the Advocate CORE Helps Me Understand My Colleagues

- Explains why a certain colleague may appear to be "opinionated" on an issue
- Provides perspective of and for others
- Shifts my own perspective toward understanding that the advocate is simply championing what they think is right (rather than trying to argue)
- Reveals the motivation behind our thoughts, feelings, and opinions

*Chapter 3*

# Changer

**Changer:** improves current systems by challenging the status quo

> *The only way that we can live, is if we grow. The only way that we can grow is if we change. The only way that we can change is if we learn. The only way we can learn is if we are exposed. And the only way that we can become exposed is if we throw ourselves out into the open. Do it. Throw yourself.*
>
> —C. JoyBell

Ok. Before you get going on chapter 3, we want to remind you of a few things. As you read, remember to use these two lenses:

- **Lens 1:** *Purpose.* What's in your CORE? Why did you get into education in the first place? It's ok if some days you wonder. You're not alone. Lens 1 is really thinking about you.

- **Lens 2:** *Perspective.* Think about your colleagues. Some are more comfortable with change than others, right? Why is that the case? How does reading this chapter help you understand them better?

Thanks for reading chapter 2 and all about the first CORE. If you liked it, tell a friend and read on. If you didn't, don't tell anyone and read on anyways. We promise (fingers crossed, behind our backs), that you'll like chapter 3 more.

**So, mom often had to *change* things up and separate us during homework time so we could "concentrate." Her additional attempt to *change* our level of focus was to make us wear these "thinking caps" (complete with a feather). Notice how thrilled we look. These simply have to be "thinking caps," right? Why else would you have, and make your children wear, these hats? A Changer "challenges the status quo." You go, mom!**

### PERSONAL STORY

Above, we defined the CORE of Changer as "improves current systems by challenging the status quo." The Changer, well, changes, how something has been previously done or used. Here's a personal story about when we both experienced change (*altering the manner in which something has been previously used . . . in this case, a garage door*). Back to our definition . . . you'll have to be the judge as to whether or not you think the story "improves" the use of the garage door, but we're quite confident it did "challenge the status quo."

Our family moved to our "forever" home just a few months before we were born. It was the summer of 1974. The home our parents and two (significantly) older brothers were in previously was small and had a tiny, one-car garage that was accessed through the alley. Our new home was newer, larger, and had an attached two-car garage with a driveway. As we grew older, we remember our father being so pleased to have an automatic garage door with an opener. It all worked well for the first eight years, but then something . . . changed.

When we were around eight years old, our neighbor Kevin was over and we had "nothing to do." As any parent knows, when our children say this, we now recognize that statement as at best difficult to understand with the closets full of toys that most kids have and at worst incredibly annoying. Anyways, we couldn't find anything to do one hot, July day. Our parents mostly sent us outside every morning with the instructions to "go play." This often led to activities like baseball, basketball, football, bike riding, exploring the nearby woods, and a few other things we can't mention here in case our parents actually read this book. That day, it was hot and so we sat in the shaded garage trying to decide what to do. This was Mistake # 1. Mistake # 2 is coming soon.

Kevin came up with the idea to use the garage door for a different purpose. To CHANGE its use from its original one, to one that would elicit more fun. His idea was simple . . . and brilliant (at least in the eyes of eight-year-old boys). With the garage door down, one of us would push the button to raise it. As the door began to rise, the other two of us would hold on to the bottom of the door and get lifted off the ground! The ride would end with us dangling a few feet off of the ground. It was tons of fun and we began laughing uncontrollably and repeating this over and over. Well, one of us (let's blame Kevin) decided that the person who pushed the button could then run over and jump onto the door with the other two and all three of us could be lifted off the ground at the same time. Good times . . . right?

Well, as the saying goes . . . "All good things must come to an end." This one ended abruptly with the door coming off the track and the motor blowing out. Weird, who would have thought that the garage door couldn't handle an extra couple hundred pounds? Not these three 8-year-olds (none of whom later became rocket scientists). Afterward, we sat on the front porch waiting for our father to come home from work, the smell of the burned-out motor still fresh in the air.

When he drove up and saw the door hanging there, his face turned red and he looked us dead in the eyes. We made sure to look straight at our shoelaces, until directed otherwise (which took about two seconds). Without a word, our friend ran to his bike and peddled home as fast as he could. We tried to explain, but there was no excuse for this type of behavior. We'll spare you the details of the consequence, but let's just say that we were raised in a strict, German household where spanking was permitted and was standard operating procedure. We didn't sit comfortably for a week or so.

So, back to our definition of Changer connected to changing the use of the garage door:

- "Improve current system" = Questionable, depends who you ask.
- "Challenge the status quo" = Nailed it.

## CHANGER DEFINED

In regards to a CORE (reminder, CORE stands for your Calling Or Reason in Education), we define a CHANGER as "someone who improves current systems by challenging the status quo." Put simply, Changers are not content with doing things the same way over and over (and over and over) again. They are constantly assessing the world and, as educators, their classroom or school, and considering new and better ways of doing things. They are energetic in their relentless pursuit of change. Remember, in the Changer's eyes, changing things means making them better. You've heard of the saying, "If it isn't broken, don't fix it." Changers haven't, or at least don't, abide by it.

Changers mean no harm, but they can definitely rub some people the wrong way. They can even offend at times with their assertiveness and desire to change things. However, the basis for the change typically includes a high level of respect for the person/persons who developed the original plan or system they'd like to tweak. **Changers appreciate the original product so much that they work to honor it by improving it, rather than scrapping it and coming up with a totally new idea.** The Innovator CORE, explained later, chooses to create new, rather than improve, the current product. So, if you're going to get offended, save it for them!

Back to Changers. They can be the best friends or worst enemies to school leaders (depending on the leader) in that they keep things fresh. School teams need them, as Changers provide the motor in the vehicle of change for staff and systems in a world where student needs are constantly evolving. We believe that the CORE of Changer can best be further defined by breaking our definition down into four main subcategories as outlined below:

- Improves Current Practices
- Dissatisfied with the Status Quo

- Holds High Expectations for Constant Improvement
- Possesses a Growth Mindset

Let's dive into the first subcategory now, with the Beatles song "Turn and Face the Strange" in mind. Educators strong in the Change CORE "turn and face the strange" in terms of making changes for kids, changes others might call "strange." Google the song. You'll be singing the song for the rest of the day. You're welcome.

## IMPROVES CURRENT PRACTICES

A Changer looks at life through the same lens as the German chemical company, BASF. (The authors are German, so we thought we'd give them a "shout out" and then go have some dumplings and sauerkraut.) Back in the late 1980s and early 1990s, BASF ran an ad campaign with the slogan, "At BASF, we don't make a lot of the products you buy, we make a lot of the products you buy better." Changers look at their individual practices, and the practices of school systems, and try to come up with better or more efficient ways to accomplish their goals.

Put on your principal hat now if you're a principal, your teacher hat if you're a teacher, your aide hat if you're an aide, and so on. Think about your own work for kids. What little changes could you make that could make a huge impact? Think about that and read on.

**Changers ask themselves, *"How can I make this better?"*** A very simple example for teachers is how they oftentimes look at teaching a lesson. Are the learning targets appropriate for this group of students? Does the plan for the instructional steps throughout the lesson need to be revisited? Do the assessments for learning support the desired outcomes, or do I need to tweak the assessment?

Doug Reeves, in his book *Leading Change in Your School: How to Conquer Myths, Build Commitment, and Get Results* (2009), writes that staff "must have a 'garden party' to pull the weeds before planting the flowers." Essentially, his findings indicate that this is a great way for teachers, for example, to look at how to dissect a lesson and "weed out" what was ineffective.

**Teacher Changers don't look at an ineffective piece of a lesson as a failure, but rather as an opportunity to make improvements for next time.** This way, next time the teacher does the lesson, with the weeds (ineffective pieces) of the lessons pulled, there'll be more room for the flowers (the parts of the lessons that rocked!). We all prefer a garden (lesson) filled with flowers (effective parts), right? Changers realize that to change things for the better, they must focus on what worked and then change the rest to make it even better.

> Educator: Choose one lesson for tomorrow that you've done before. Take five minutes to reflect on any changes, even minor ones, that you could make this year to it to make it better. When delivering the lesson tomorrow, while the students are immersed in the part that you changed, enjoy it. Their learning more today because you made the change!
>
> Leader: You know you have teachers who are Changers, and teachers who haven't changed a thing since before they created sliced bread (which was 1928, BTW). Approach your very best teacher and ask them how they change their lessons each year to meet the needs of their ever-changing students. Then, consider, how could this information be modeled and shared with others.

The key here is that **the Changer takes a real, honest look at their own professional practice and their results.** "The source of creative breakthroughs is learning from and about practice, not theory" (Fullan, 2011). Fullan takes it further by talking about the importance of drawing conclusions from what you've learned from your own practices or from others and then expanding on them. The Changer analyzes the effectiveness of whatever change they've made, reflecting on its' impact on student achievement, and then decides what of that change is worth keeping and building on, and what should be discarded. This behavior is key for successful Changers.

Changer CORE Steps:

Step one: Reflect on practices.
Step two: Make changes.
Step three: Keep what works and toss what doesn't.
Step four: Repeat.

From a school or district level, Changers look at programs and systems and find ways to make them more efficient or evolve with the needs of the customer, typically the students. This can be very intimidating and challenging for most people as it includes taking on large-scale projects that can take months or years to work through. There is a high level of commitment, perseverance, and patience that is required to see through big systems change. However, Changers see the big picture and intentionally determine each necessary step along the path to accomplish the end goal.

At one of the schools where I was an elementary school principal, student growth in reading, especially for lower performing readers, was a focus. And, well, it's likely a focus of many schools all over the country! Reading, it's kind of a big deal. One change that our school made was to give teachers a structured opportunity to regularly talk with grade-level colleagues around answering specific questions about readers of whom they were the most concerned. The coaches, the principal, and, at the beginning of the school year, the previous years' teachers were present. This isn't rocket science or I wouldn't have come up with it, but still . . . . These were either lower performing readers or readers who were not making their expected growth, and they needed us to change.

We put a structure in place for teachers by grade level to meet to discuss those students individually by name. The conversations could be incredibly powerful. Think about it. Sitting around the table were several teachers with various experiences as reading instructors, a reading coach with a diverse background both as a former teacher and as someone connected with other reading coaches in the district who had knowledge of best reading practices, and the (incredibly good-looking) principal who had a vertical view of readers as they progressed through the grades.

While I'd be lying if I said that all teachers were really excited to come to each meeting (shocker, I know), I do know that these conversations made an impact on many students, one at a time. Additionally, during reading walk-throughs (short, unannounced classroom observations of student learning) the rest of the year, I'd focus on making sure to sit next to the previously discussed couple of students in each room during reading time to check on their progress. Principals: You're (hopefully) in classrooms anyways. It takes exactly zero extra minutes to talk with the student you had discussed in the meeting about reading progress. And, well, when teachers know you're going to do it, they're more likely to implement what was discussed at the meeting. Accountability 101.

So, what happened? We saw results for kids in terms of improved reading scores! As we all know, change can be hard. No one wants "another meeting." However, when the change means growth in student learning, I'd call that a win for change and, more importantly, for students.

## DISSATISFIED WITH THE STATUS QUO

**Changers know that change is necessary in order to improve.** For Changers, it can be scarier when things stay the same. In general, they believe that past practices, no matter how proven at the time, become stagnant and less effective over time. They believe that as learners need change, so must we. Changers challenge the norm, the way things have always been done. A key component in Changers is that they can often see the NEED for change before others, perhaps even before data is showing trends that would support altering a current practice.

**Change can seem risky at times, but when you think about it, NOT changing can be even riskier.** "Change is hard, and people vary in their capacity to handle it. They also vary in their perceptions in what risks are worth taking—though there are always risks to both leaving the status quo as it is and taking action to implement change" (Benson, 2015). Educators don't often consider the risks of leaving the status quo as is. There are just as many (and at times more) risks to NOT changing.

My second school counselor position was at an urban, diverse, comprehensive high school of around 1,500 students. At the time, our student services department was pretty well staffed with five school counselors and a school social worker (SSW). With a high-needs school consisting of mostly low-income, transient students and all of the struggles that accompany that, there was plenty to do. Over time, budget cuts and district initiatives forced a change to the staffing assignments.

During one of the first years in my position as department chairperson, we lost our social worker position. Now, the need for an experienced, effective SSW was definitely still present, but we had to face the fact that we would not have anyone in that role moving forward.

As a department leader, I approached this issue the way I did with most challenges. I approached it from a positive, problem-solving angle and included my colleagues in every step of the process. We met at the end of the school year leading up to the change and again during the summer to break down the issue and identify potential solutions. We came up with a few things we all agreed upon. First, there would be no change in the needs of the students we served so we had to figure out a way to continue the high-quality, timely, proactive, and responsive services we had always provided. Second, outsourcing the student needs to other SSWs in the district was not feasible (nor, in our minds, ethical). Third, we all had different comfort levels in taking on the duties of a traditional SSW.

Now, I had a few things going for me as we entered this far from ideal change. First, I had a background in social work. I had earned a bachelor's degree in social work, had been a state-certified social worker, and had worked in the field for eight years prior to becoming a school counselor. This by no means replaced the need we had for one or lessened the high level of respect I have for the skill set of SSWs (my wife is a SSW, as a matter of fact, and I don't want to sleep on the couch tonight!). Second, due to a highly overutilized past SSW, I had taken on delivering many of the social work–related needs of the 350 students on my caseload for the last two years or so. Third, and most importantly, I had the experience in both roles and the clarity to see the numerous similarities in the social worker and school counselor role, at least as structured in our school and district.

So the decision was made that we, as school counselors, had the responsibility to build our capacity around social work competencies in order to effectively serve our students, families, and school. We didn't have to be experts and we would learn when to reach out to the professionals we had around us. Again, I knew going in that this would end up being a more comfortable transition than my colleagues did. They entered the endeavor with some expected apprehension, but soon realized that their counseling training and skills were more easily transferable than expected. It took about two years of focused professional development, support from district social workers, and regular collaboration to learn from one another, but we were able to provide quality supports and services to our students. Since the change had been made to remove the SSW position, we had to make changes in our service delivery model. It was a needed and necessary one for our students.

> It is my responsibility to be an ally for my students and families of color, of disability, economically disadvantaged, language diversity, etc., in breaking down the barriers that exist in our school systems. (CM, elementary teacher

## HOLDS HIGH EXPECTATIONS FOR CONSTANT IMPROVEMENT

Changers have high expectations of themselves and the professionals around them to constantly be looking for ways to make their service to students better. If you are tasked to work with a Changer, be ready for those same standards to be placed onto you. If you're prepared for this and accept the challenge, positive results are sure to follow. Even in projects that may not succeed to the extent originally hoped since Changers typically make lofty goals for themselves, there will be much to be learned throughout the journey. **When working with Changers, know this: the more out of your comfort zone you are with the work, the higher the possible chance for success**.

Changers bring energy along with those high expectations. They are motivated by one goal: making something that is good, even better. Instead of being put off by their passion and effort, take a leap of faith and go along for the ride with them. We discuss perspective and trust a lot in this book. This is a perfect example of getting comfortable with other people's passions (in this case, the passion for change) and trusting them to the point where you will allow yourself to follow them even without being fully sold on it yourself.

As an educator, you already know that every staff person brings certain qualities to the team and that we will all achieve more TOGETHER than we would on our own. And, we will achieve more by TRUSTING each other rather than battling each other in attempts to gain agreement. **The Changer**

**knows that agreeing on everything rarely gets you anywhere.** Take a moment and reflect on that.

Think of any major school-wide accomplishment that you have experienced. We highly doubt that all stakeholders were 100 percent on board from start to finish (no, wait, we're actually *positive* about that). No, there were hurdles along the way and some who disagreed with the change. There was doubt, worry, confusion, lack of buy-in, hesitation, and even times when some wanted to give up.

Change is a messy process. You can choose to stay "clean" and make no real improvements, or you can roll up your sleeves to get "dirty" and reap the rewards. For the sake of your students, we say, get filthy.

| Educator: The next time you are faced with a change that makes you uncomfortable, take a deep breath and realize that feeling this discomfort is normal (and is actually a good sign, a sign that you're growing). |
| --- |
| Leader: Identify your Changers early, then go to them often.......especially when things seem to be going well. Remember, they see ahead of the curve. Take advantage of their eyesight. |

As mentioned earlier, Changers honor the hard work of others who have created strong, proven plans and systems before them. Staff need to see that the **Changer is not proposing change to upset or unsettle the adults, but rather as a response to meet the needs of kids**. Remember, they have high expectations for constant improvement.

All too often in education, we hear ourselves make statements about everything being about what's best for kids. Then, do you know what happens? The adults (us) get in the way. We begin to take things personally or disagree with a school initiative based on *who* proposed it or the details of *what* is being proposed. Said another way, we get in the way of the change.

If you catch yourself or a colleague listing off all the reasons you feel a certain change will not work, STOP and ask yourself where this is really coming from. If any of the answers have to do with adults and not kids, take a step back and reassess your position. Change is hard enough as it is, let's not get in our own way and make it even more difficult!

## POSSESSES A GROWTH MINDSET

"The growth mindset is based off the belief in change. Nothing is better than seeing people find their way to things they value" (Dweck, 2006).

Changers have a growth mindset. Changers, like any of our COREs, use their skills and beliefs to reach goals, of course, and also to be personally fulfilled. **Changers know that adapting with kids and the world is the key component to success and feeling professionally and personally fulfilled.**

As mentioned earlier and as you are aware, change does not come easily for some. It's why, when you search on Google about the difficulty of change, 81.4 million hits pop up in .68 seconds. It's quicker to just keep doing things the way you've always done them. And, you're an educator, so you likely feel that you don't have the time for certain changes or improvements. However, part of the growth mindset that Changers possess is the understanding that while the process will initially take a little more time and will have ups and downs, it will be worth it in the end.

Failures are a huge part of the learning and growth process that occurs in order to even have the potential of finding success in a change. Unfortunately, it's that fear of failure that keeps some from attempting a change at all. Educators strong in the **Changer CORE, however, reflect on what worked and what didn't, then make adjustments moving forward.** They don't perseverate on the mistakes, but rather embrace them as the means to get closer to the answers and results that they are searching for (the near-perfect schedule that an administrator creates, the dynamic lesson that a teacher engages students in, the thoughtful plan a counselor puts in place to support a student, etc.). Changers tend to be very reflective, and then intentional in how they respond. This is all part of having a growth mindset.

Changers are open-minded. They are the ones who sometimes sit silently in a meeting or a professional development activity and are constantly considering what is being discussed. An observer would say that they can "see their wheels turning" as the Changer contemplates how and when to insert their thoughts into the conversation. Instead of hearing an idea involving a proposed change and asking "Why," the Changer hears it and responds, "Why not?" (more to come on this concept in the Innovator chapter).

We know that's not rocket science stuff here, but think about it for a moment. It's not that a Changer goes along with every idea of how to make something different or potentially better. That's not the case at all. Rather, they simply approach it a different way. Again, **Changers take the "why not?" approach and create an opinion about a proposed change based on how they answer the question.** They don't change just for changes sake, they change because it's better for kids.

Educator: Are you frustrated with some procedure or classroom routine that simply isn't producing the results it used to? You've recognized it. Now change it. Go. Do. Tomorrow your frustration will turn into joy (or at least something better than frustration.)

Leader: The next time a staff person approaches you with an idea of how to improve something, genuinely listen and trust them. If you are "on the fence" and would normally say "No," this time, just…..say…… "YES."

Like anything, times change, but often our systems do not. Time changes slowly. Change to where the same lesson, the same homework, or the same consequence just doesn't have the same impact on students like it used to. This has been glaringly obvious the last decade or so. Kids are growing up differently than we did as kids. (Oh boy, we're starting to sound like our parents.) It's true, though. In this digital world of cell phones and screen time, kids are simply used to a different level of ongoing feedback and stimulation. Our lessons have to be prepared for that and delivered with that in mind. **So, don't stick with what you know. Instead, stick with what you know today's kids need.**

One such example is how schools, teachers and administrators, respond to behavior issues. When we attended school as youngsters (from the late 1970s into the early 1990s—don't do the math on our age, please), there was really only one way to respond to behavior issues: discipline. As much as strict, consistent, punitive responses work for some students, it's not as broadly effective today as it used to be.

Being the principal at an alternative education high school forced me to look at the traditionally used punitive responses that our school, and district, had used for years. When I started, the district gave me an at-a-glance discipline response chart. It listed each offense with the consequence. Its intentions were good and necessary. It aimed to offer administrators an idea of what punishment "fit the crime," as well as provided consistency throughout all schools in a district of around 10,000 students at the time.

What didn't sit well with me, and maybe this was my social worker and counselor background, was the exclusive focus on responses to behaviors. The good news was, it didn't sit well with my district either, and a real focus had already begun to investigate how to TEACH the behaviors we wanted to see, rather than punish the ones we didn't.

This is where Restorative Practices (RP) enter the picture. RP is well known and so I won't dive very deeply into it, but it is based on the concept of creating bonds between adults and kids to where both feel an obligation to each other to conduct themselves in certain ways. It's about creating a family-like atmosphere in which all feel loved and cared for, but where expectations are clear. In a strong restorative atmosphere, students WANT to do the right thing and feel bad when they don't, not just because they want to do better for themselves, but because they feel obligated to their peers and teachers.

It is based on the idea that there needs to be a relationship built between kids and adults, and kids and their peers, so that there is something to repair when harm has been done. So, before the story goes any further, you can already see the dramatic change that would need to occur over time when we consider the movement from punitive responses toward this more proactive, growth mindset–type approach of RP.

Anyways, to say implementing RP in any district is an easy change would be far from the truth. As mentioned previously, change can be uncomfortable and it is generally much easier to keep doing what you're doing. In our case however, what we had always been doing just wasn't working anymore.

Luckily, most of the 750 or so teachers in the district were looking for other options to improve their classroom environments. It was time for a change. Through an RP workgroup consisting of representatives from every level and school, school board information sessions, an intentional professional development plan, building teams, parent information efforts, and contracted supports from the experts at the International Institute of Restorative Practices (IIRP), we were able to slowly and intentionally integrate these ideals into our schools. Over the past few years, our school and district have shown decreases in school behavioral referrals, suspensions, expulsions, and recidivism, along with increases in student engagement and a sense of belonging.

Dweck wrote, "Change can be tough, but I never heard anyone say it wasn't worth it. Maybe they're just rationalizing, the way people who've gone through a painful initiation (difficult change) say it was worth it. But people who've changed can tell you how their lives have been enhanced. They can tell you about things they have now that they wouldn't have had, and ways they feel now that they wouldn't have felt" (p. 246).

Depending on the age of the students you work with, some will be able to communicate the positive impact a change made by an adult at school had on their lives. For most students, however, they won't have the skills to clearly communicate that. But, does it matter? Students across the district in the scenario we just described are infinitely better off because adults had a growth mindset approach to change. Do you?

Change can be difficult, but it's almost always worth it!

I believed that my students could change the world. They have and they still are in ways I could never imagine. (Judy F., high school teacher)

## SUMMARY

We define a person who is strong in the Changer CORE as someone who "improves current systems by challenging the status quo." We believe that those staff in the school where you work each day have the following four characteristics in common:

- Improves Current Practices
- Dissatisfied with the Status Quo
- Holds High Expectations for Constant Improvement
- Possesses a Growth Mindset

One misconception we've attempted to help you recognize is the belief that Changers want to change things just for the sake of changing them, that they are always looking to throw out what was done in the past and start fresh with something new. What we propose is quite the contrary. **Changers appreciate the original product so much that they work to honor it by improving it, rather than scrapping it and coming up with a totally new idea.**

So, the next time someone proposes a change to something in your school, consider the potential for that change with an open mind and an open heart. **Changers are the motor in the vehicle of improvement for staff and systems in a world where student needs are constantly evolving.** They provide the spark for school teams to recognize what students need and take the necessary next steps.

Lastly, know that a key component to Changers is that they can often see (or hear) the need for change well before others. For you old-timers out there (us included), think of the character Radar on the show MASH from the 1970s and early 1980s, who could hear the military helicopters coming around the bend. For you youngsters out there, Google it. He could hear change was on the way before anyone else.

In the end, change can seem risky at times, but when you think about it, NOT changing can be even riskier. The Changer gets that. Do you?

## Perspective-Taking Scenario

You are a supervisory aide at an elementary or middle school. Your duties include recess supervision. For years, you and three of your colleagues have walked the playground area, assisting students as needed during recess time. Admittedly, at times you have somewhat lengthy conversations (not necessarily about school-related topics) with your colleagues, which if you're being honest has impacted how focused you are on keeping students safe on the playground. But, hey, you rationalized, I had a fun weekend and I want to tell my colleagues about it.

The principal notices this (the fun weekends you've been apparently having and talking about) and decides to assign zones of coverage for each of the four aides, which involves each of you needing to stand in your own assigned area. She explains what she has observed and the need for this change. She tells the group that she believes that each aide having their own designated location on the playground will help reduce student misbehaviors because the adult will be better able to address any minor issues immediately in part because of their proximity to the students.

When she shares this change with the group, no one has any questions or comments. However, in the parking lot after school, one of the aides questions why the change is necessary because her perspective is that the status quo has been working fine. You are the other aide. You agree with this change that the principal has made. . . . What do you say?

## CORE Questions to Consider

1. When was the last time you initiated a significant change regarding your profession/position? What were the results?
2. Think of a time when a colleague took a risk and tried to change something and was unsuccessful. How did it change how you viewed them?
3. If you got your boss' job tomorrow, what one change would you make your very first day on the job? Why? Now, assuming you won't actually get your boss' job tomorrow (and who in their right mind would want that job anyway, right?), what could you do in your current role to support making that same change successful?

## We Dare You Challenge

Think about a few things you'd like to change about some aspect of your job, things that add (or will soon add) gray hair to your head. Select just one of those things. Now, come up with three actions you could take to make this change your current reality. Write those actions below:

1. _____

2. _____

3. _____

Now do it. Or, do you have stock in (insert hair product company here)?

**Now What?/Action Steps**

If this is your CORE, you should use it for the following actions:

- Know and live that there is always a better way to do something
- Approach your school leader to suggest improvements
- Consistently monitor and reflect on your practice
- Be comfortable out of your comfort zone

Why Every Team Needs Someone with the CHANGER CORE

- To keep things fresh and rejuvenate those who are stagnant
- To recognize that we must always shift to meet changing student needs
- To see the change that is needed first
- To show others the benefits of having the courage to change

How Identifying People with the CHANGER CORE Helps My School Leader

- Models the necessity to look for change
- Gets others to see the pitfalls of complacency
- Acts as a pilot who then grows to impact an even wider audience
- Keeps things fresh, new, and exciting

How Understanding the CHANGER CORE Helps Me Understand My Colleagues

- Provides safety in participating in the change
- Understands their role as the risk-taker
- Comfort knowing there is someone volunteering to try something new
- Realize that they are actually looking for improvement

*Chapter 4*

# Character-Builder

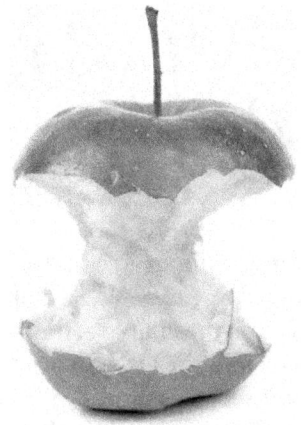

**Character-Builder:** moves beyond academics to focus on the whole child and creating better people.

> *Watch your thoughts; they become words. Watch your words; they become actions. Watch your actions; they become habits. Watch your habits; they become character. Watch your character; it becomes your destiny.*
>
> —Unknown

**So, when we were kids, our mom dressed us the same every day. And, when we say every day, we mean every . . . single . . . day. The only potential difference was, as pictured above, the color of the stripes on our socks. As if that wasn't enough, she also made sure that, even on the hottest of summer days, those socks were pulled all the way to the bottoms of our shorts. Talk about character-building!**

## PERSONAL STORY

Above, we defined the CORE of Character-Builder as someone who "moves beyond academics to focus on the whole child and creating better people." Well, in our lives the people who built our character were our parents, teachers, coaches, friends, and neighbors . . . oh, and of course, our two older brothers.

Looking back, it is now obvious to us to see that we took the "advice" and "guidance" of our two older brothers way too seriously. This is mostly true for the second oldest brother of the family. We'll call him Jeff (since that's his real name and this is finally our chance to expose him for some of his questionable—or were they borderlining straight up inappropriate—actions). Note to the reader: We're just being funny here. No need to worry. Note to Jeff: We told you years ago that payback was coming. Even then, we didn't know exactly how. The time has come. Also, while you are enjoying reading this story, know that there will be others coming in future chapters.

Jeff was, and still is, seven years older than us (that's kinda how time works). Growing up in our family, that meant that when our parents weren't around, he was in charge of "taking care of us." In his mind, that meant that we were to stay out of his way unless he needed us around for his own amusement. Admittedly, this at first glance doesn't seem to sound too much different from what many of you who have older siblings experienced when you were kids. But, wait for it.

We won't get too far into explaining that except for saying that it included some harmless (in his mind) teasing and torture (sidenote: Can torture be harmless?). Note that he's now (somehow) a responsible, respected adult who supervises many others, so we'll only share some stories that won't jeopardize his employment or get him tossed into prison. He is also happily married with a son of his own, and admittedly was then, and is now, an all around good guy. But, don't tell him we said that.

On with the story. One major piece of Jeff's repertoire was embarrassing us in front of our friends. He is the older brother, after all. This could include driving us places and honking the car horn at girls from our school while announcing that we were in love with them (further details coming in the "Connector" chapter), to "beating us up" in front of our friends with just his pointer finger (a skill we may or may not have passed on to our own children). It will go down in history being known as "the one finger treatment." That's all we'll say about that. Finally, Jeff's eyes would light up when he would hear that we were having a sleepover. This type of event offered multiple opportunities for him to get creative with, and perfect, his techniques regarding harassing his younger brothers, and as an additional gift their friends too (bonus).

Let's talk more about sleepovers as that's the heart of this story. Growing up, we had typical sleepovers for the time (early 1980s). We would have two to three friends over for the night. We'd mostly play sports outside, then come inside at dark to play Atari (Google it Millennials and Generation Zs), or later Nintendo. Board games and cards were also typical events at our sleepovers. We would all get our sleeping bags spread out on the family room floor where the only television was and have a snack or play some handheld electronic games as the night grew later and our parents went to bed for the evening.

Over the years, Jeff built a reputation with our friends as someone who would tease and, again, borderline torture us when they slept over. Looking back, why they kept agreeing to come over for sleepovers is mind-boggling. While we were sleeping, he would do things like (and, no, you can't make this stuff up):

- put toothpaste in our ears (*a gross way to wake up*)
- paint our fingernails (*an embarrassing way to wake up*)
- cut chunks out of our hair (*a shocking way to wake up*)
- draw earrings on us with permanent marker (*a classy way to wake up*)
- tie the top of our sleeping bags shut so we couldn't get out (*a confusing way to wake up*)
- set and hide multiple hidden alarm clocks off throughout the night (*an annoying way to wake up*)
- and his favorite by far . . . draw on our faces with marker (usually in the form of mustaches, beards, eye glasses, eyebrows, etc.) (*a fun-for-every-one-else way to wake up*)

We would all wake up in the morning feeling oddly like we'd been disturbed while trying to sleep, only to look in the mirror to see what damage had been done. And, by the way, toothpaste is REALLY hard to get out of your ears when it's been drying for several hours. We'd suggest NOT trying this at home (or any of the other things mentioned above, for that matter).

Now, we did come up with a variety of clever ways of combating his attacks, but perhaps we'll share those later. The point of this story is that no matter how delusional it may seem, Jeff would tell us over the years (even now as adults) that it was his duty to do these things to us. In response to our questions about why, he would always say, **"Hey, it built character."** And so there it is.

We went through all of this from our big brother to build our character. Neither of us are too sure about that, but it's his story, and he's sticking to it. So, "thank you, Jeff." We think.

We hope that you too had experiences as a child that built your character, that made you the person and educator that you are today. We also hope that, for your own emotional and physical well-being, you couldn't relate to our story about Jeff! Our final hope is that you can relate to our definition of the Character-Builder CORE and how it helps you with your own work for kids, and to better understand the work of your colleagues.

## CHARACTER-BUILDER DEFINED

In regards to a CORE, we define a Character-Builder as someone who "moves beyond academics to focus on the whole child and creating better people." After all, what's the point of educating kids if we're not creating better people who eventually go out to help create a better world? (That's a rhetorical question.) Education is about more than academics, as Character-Builders realize and act on each day. They constantly keep in the front of their mind **the end goal of young people becoming the high-quality human beings that they have the potential to be**. Character-Builders are unwavering in their efforts to maximize the chances of helping students to become more caring, respectful, responsible, trustworthy, fair, and overall good citizens.

We believe that every single person in education has an element of this in them, of course. However, for certain individuals, this is their CORE, their Calling Or Reason they're in Education. Character-Builders want to live their own lives knowing that when they leave this world, it's a better place than when they found it. As educators, though, they want to multiply that impact by creating kids, every one of them, who do the same.

**Character-Builders are big picture people, comfortable with the long-term commitment needed to produce real results**. They understand that results to prove their efforts may not be easily quantified, but are satisfied knowing that they are having a lifelong impact by creating better people. Character-Builders know that, through their efforts as an educator, years down the road when they hear about how and what their former students are doing with their lives, nearly always it will be something that makes them feel proud to have been involved in their education. They'll know, deep down, that they played a part in that former students success in life well beyond what they taught them academically.

**Character-Builders find a way to connect academic learning to the real world** (similar to those educators strong in the CORE of what we call "Preparers," which we will discuss later). However, Character-Builders do so through a lens of helping their students to become overall better people. So, not in the sense of being academically ready for college or being successful in a certain career field, but more the qualities and characteristics that we all look for in people we want to surround ourselves with in our own lives. Which one do you think is more important? That's also a rhetorical question, but one worth considering for a moment.

These people of strong character end up also being the ones who we want to hire, want on our team at work, desire to be our bosses, or even want to be our friends beyond the job. For those of you who are parents, think of the kids you want your own children to hang around with. Those are the kids we're talking about in this chapter. Those are the future Character-Builders.

*Sidenote: Character-Builders are probably NOT the kids who have an older brother like ours who does some of the things described earlier in this chapter. Against all odds though, the authors believe they've still somehow managed to become Character-Builders themselves. We hope, however, that your path to Character-Building doesn't involve toothpaste in your ear while you sleep . . .*

We believe that the CORE of Character-Builders can best be further defined by breaking our definition down into four main subcategories as outlined below:

- Whole Child View
- Focus on Character Development
- Teaching of Real-World Skills
- Future Over Present

## WHOLE CHILD VIEW

Character-Builders realize that the main purpose of schools is not to create academically competent students, but rather to develop people of strong character. Now, we know this statement may not sit well with some of you. You might be thinking . . . students are in school to learn, right? I mean, they need to know their alphabet, how to read, their multiplication facts, and how to write. These academically focused aspects of a child's schooling are indeed necessary for students to be "ready" for tomorrow, next week, and all of the next years in their classes. The Character-Builder recognizes that, but also sees *beyond* that.

We talked in the introduction of this book about "Stepping Back to See the Whole Orchard." In that section, we shared the importance of removing ourselves as much as is possible from the day-to-day stressors of the job to see the bigger picture, the reason we work so hard in the first place. Character-Builders do just that. They know that education is not just about academics. They know that what a student needs to be successful in the future is changing each day, and it's beyond purely memorizing information and getting good grades in their classes. So, it IS about academics, but it's also about so much more.

Educator: Did your last lesson or unit contain any component of character-building? Likely not. What will you add to your current or next lesson or unit to include it?

Leader: When you consider your staff, do certain people stick out as those who regularly embed character-building into their interactions with students? Set up a meeting with that person to discuss this strength and brainstorm suggestions as to how they could share this skill with other staff members.

**Character-Builders recognize the importance of spending a lot of time early in the year on relationship-building and classroom/school culture before diving into content**. They also know that it's necessary to continue to do so ongoing throughout the year. They know that reaching their long-term goals for student achievement means gaining buy-in from students in a real and authentic way. They are the ones in your school who may, from the perspective of some staff members, seem to start the year "having too much fun" and "just playing games" with their students the first couple of days.

You might wonder, "What is going on in the classroom next door when the class erupts in laughter a few times a day?" Well, don't allow that to be a rhetorical question. We'd suggest you find out and consider incorporating some of that into your own professional practice if you don't already (*unless it involves marker mustaches while kids are sleeping. And, BTW, if kids are sleeping in your presence, as an educator you've got different, much more significant problems*).

**Character-Builders are not light on content, they just know the foundational pieces of relationship-building and trust that needs to be solidified before working through the essential academic pieces**. And, aren't activities in your classroom (or school or district) to build relationships in your classrooms kinda, oh, what's the word . . . oh yeah . . . FUN? Couldn't we all use a little more fun these days?

> My purpose is to help kids develop a healthy relationship with fitness and exercise. I want students to be exposed to a variety of lifetime activities with the hope that they find something that "sticks" and peaks their interest enough that they will continue with the particular activity outside of school. (Karen, high school physical education teacher)

Johnson (2017) writes, "If we are truly teaching learners and preparing them for a future not yet written, then we need to consider the critical need for all students to receive a viable education that not only includes core content but also purposeful integration of the 4 C's. It is not enough to retain knowledge and information." The 4 Cs Johnson refers to are: Critical thinking, Communication skills, Collaboration and team building, and Creativity and innovation.

The point she makes about education being about far more than retaining information is a key one. Research shows over and over that this skill of "doing school," as far as getting good grades, is by itself not going to get our students very far. Students deserve so much more than that. They deserve the 4 Cs that Johnson describes. Stop. Think for a moment. As an educator regardless of your role, what opportunities do you provide your students for the 4 Cs? What could you do tomorrow to increase the focus on one of the Cs?

We've noticed that most books for educators focus on academic results (as they arguably should), as well as collaboration, change, culture, evaluation, and so on. But, a CORE of ours, even before you can improve these things in your classroom or school, is **focusing on students as people, not just learners**. After all, we want them to be caring, respectful, responsible, trustworthy, fair, and overall good citizens. While focusing on the whole child through character-building techniques will in the end impact these things listed above (like the almighty test score), it's difficult to directly connect the impact since it's not linear. Perhaps this is why many schools across all levels don't focus on character-building enough. Consider that further as we share a story with you.

As a principal, I gave many tours of our school to prospective families. One stands out beyond all others. The parents toured with their child, who had autism. The family was considering moving from out of state, and were quite admirably basing most of their decision of where in southeastern Wisconsin to live on what school would best serve their child's needs. Without getting into details, I was confident in the abilities of our school staff that we'd be the best fit for him. Still, I knew that with his needs he would stretch our staff to places they (and I) had not yet been.

During the tour, having a clear sense that our school was best for him and for us, I tried to highlight the many reasons he would be successful in our school and tried to be especially responsive to parents' questions and concerns. I felt like, looking forward many years down the road, he would have the best chance at making the world a better place as a result of attending our school. I also knew that, despite the short-term challenges that he might provide day-to-day as we learned how to best support his needs, we'd grow stronger as a staff as a result of working with him.

The great news is that the family chose our school. The even better news is that he thrived in our school for years to come. Perhaps the best news is the student also had a significant impact on the other students in our school, in more ways than I could have imagined. In this manner, much like the characteristics that have been described in this chapter, I saw the big picture of the mutual benefit of having this boy attend our school. We for sure built his character through our instruction of curriculum but more so by developing his social and "life" skills through other learning experiences that he had. And, most certainly he built ours up even more.

While the whole child view is one major component of the Character-Builder as we've described in the previous paragraphs, developing the character of students is a second main category that we'd like to discuss further.

## FOCUS ON CHARACTER DEVELOPMENT

Much has been written in education in the more recent years regarding character development. When you think "character development" in schools, you likely think about things like creating caring, respectful, responsible students as well as what was mentioned in the previous section.

Here's a related quote for you to consider: "A focus on success in life means that, beyond teaching the three R's, we must also teach character, emotional intelligence, responsibility, and an appreciation for the complexity of human diversity" (Hoerr, 2013). Respectfully, and perhaps somewhat dependent on the grade or content that you teach, how much of this do you do each day?

Character-Builders realize and embrace the fact that it is now the role of the school, and each staff member in it, to assist parents/guardians in developing the character of our youth. We can waste time debating whose responsibility this should be (usually with ideas of "how it used to be" in our heads), but it would be more efficient to accept this as reality and focus our energy on helping grow good people. Regardless of a child's home life, it's our role as educators to develop student's character through our interactions with them each day. It's really not in some curriculum, it's in every single interaction. The sooner educators take personal accountability for the outcomes of students in all facets of their growth and development, the better off we will all be.

So, if helping to build character is so important, why don't more people in education focus on it? First off, we'd submit that there are actually a huge percentage of educators who do; they just do so in subtle ways. We all know that **the best teachers artfully weave life lessons into their academic lessons.** The bottom line, the word that most educators use to answer this question, is "time" (an obvious lack thereof). There are also so many political pressures present in education today that focus on test results and overall academic achievement measures, which makes any shift away from that a very difficult and risky one.

Even school leaders, who are generally former teachers, know the importance of building strong character in kids. But things change when they are now responsible for not only the achievement scores of their individual classroom like before, but also the achievement scores of *every* student in *every* classroom in the school. What was a slightly risky change to focus on allocating more time to character development earlier in their career as a classroom teacher, now just became a very large gamble as a school administrator. This is a gamble that not many leaders are willing to take, as they get consumed by test data and making plans to improve it. We believe, though, that in this case the risk will almost certainly reap rewards in the long term.

Educator: When a student has a behavioral issue, do you most often give punishment as a consequence? Does that change the behavior and build the student's character? Or, just simply temporarily stop the undesired behavior? Instead, how could you build up their character through proactive and positive interactions for long term results?

Leader: Tomorrow, seek out the student who is a "frequent flyer" in your office. Get to know them for reasons other than the norm. Compliment them when you notice them being respectful, responsible, trustworthy, etc. Then, enjoy seeing them in your office less.

Part of building character is failure. We discussed in the CHANGER chapter about trusting that risk-taking and failure are part of the learning process and keys for growth. Modeling this is so important for student learning as well. **Students need to understand that they should not be afraid to fail, but rather have confidence in knowing that it is a necessary part of the learning process.** Hoerr wrote, "We must also teach the virtues of grit—tenacity, perseverance, and the ability to never give up" (2013). Creating a safe place to fail is all part of this. Teachers must create a space where students feel comfortable trying new things, knowing full well that they may not succeed on the first, second, or even seventh (no, that's not a typo) try. And, that is ok!

The real lesson learned might not end up being a tangible one. The most powerful lesson might actually be a student building perseverance and grit, essentially, the part of their character that will help them continue to try when things become difficult. Think for a moment about yourself, your own character, if you will. What experiences made you the person you are today?

Seriously, stop and think . . . Likely, the answers that you just thought about weren't things that were necessarily positive or even came easy. More than likely, they were things that you had to work for, you had to earn. That's grit, and that's what a Character-Builder teaches.

> Teaching grit can be difficult for educators because the concept appears to run counter to the caring school environments that we all strive for. It is very important that students enjoy learning and want to come to school, but teaching grit necessarily means that students will experience, and perhaps embrace—some frustration and pain. We do our students no favors if we fail to prepare them for the real world because they do not know how to respond to frustration and failure. (Hoerr, 2013)

So, teachers, what are you doing tomorrow to give your students the gift of grit? If tomorrow is Sunday, then it's ok to say "nothing." But otherwise . . .

During my first year as principal at an alternative education high school where developing character is a key part of our focus for our students, I recall a parent approaching me after the graduation ceremony. He was most interested in the statements that I had made about our students being resilient. He wanted to know more about that. I explained that our students were "at-risk" students, coming from challenging environments and that the key component that I believe they all possess was resiliency, the ability to withstand and recover from difficult conditions, the very ones they spent their lives in every day.

During the ceremony that night, I had also proclaimed in my speech that these types of individuals are, in my belief, those who have the best chance of becoming successful adults. I defined success as being happy and fulfilled in life. A simple definition, but truer in my mind than using extraneous or materialistic factors like how much money they'd make or what job title they'd have.

During that conversation with the parent, he also challenged me on my statements about my belief that these at-risk, often low-performing (academically), students could possibly be more "successful" than those from the two traditional comprehensive high schools in our district where they were exposed to a broader, more rigorous (in some ways) curriculum and which had higher standardized test scores each year.

My stance was that some, not all, of the students from traditional high schools that he referred to could indeed retain and perhaps apply things that they learned. However, I believed that they were not accustomed to failure or the same struggles in life that my students had experienced, and so I questioned whether many of the students from the traditional high school setting possessed the grit required to remain focused on achieving their goals when times got tough (basically, having a strong enough character to do so).

What we were really debating was, what are the measures of being "successful" in school? Is it retention of content knowledge (test scores and grades) or growth of their character? The author's stance is that **a successful person needs strong character including grit in order to fully learn and utilize the academic content required in today's schools.** So, we are saying both, but that the character part predicates the content piece. Said another way, while most students can, if they so choose, succeed in "the game of school" (completing their homework, getting good grades, etc.), it's only the students who have a strong character that succeed in "the game of life" (being happy, productive, contributing members of society—*who don't hang their little brothers' friends' bikes in trees for fun . . . Jeff*).

## TEACHING OF REAL-WORLD SKILLS

Character-Builders firmly believe that the building of a strong, trusting learning environment is THE component of their classroom that is required in order to achieve the academic results they desire for their students. It is these foundational pieces that support academic learning and also mimic the skills needed to thrive later, in the "real world." Character-Builders realize that to succeed in any postsecondary arena, these "real-world" skills may be more crucial than content knowledge. Woah! Back up the bus. Did you just read that correctly? Yes, you did. We said "more crucial" than content knowledge.

Teachers who are Character-Builders realize that the most impactful "lessons" they can offer their students are connected to skills they will need well beyond the classroom. Said differently, if you're teaching something to your students and you hope they don't ask, *"What does this have to do with anything I'll need in the real world?"* then it's time for you to reevaluate your lesson and perhaps talk to your school leaders about what you're teaching. True, these real-world skills won't be reflected on many report cards because they're hard to assess. But we respectfully respond, WHO CARES?!?!?!

Educator: Do you model the characteristics such as respect, caring and fairness that you want to see in your students every single day?

Leader: How do you support educators implementing character-building into their work with kids? When is the last time you discussed it as a staff or department?

We know that all educators, regardless of your role, can be Character-Builders. In fact, some of the most impactful Character-Builders might not be teachers at all. No disrespect intended (especially because one of the authors is a teacher!). Instead, it's difficult (or if we're being honest, nearly impossible) for teachers to connect with every student each day in a meaningful way beyond what we need to teach them. So, if you're an educator who is not a classroom teacher, know that you can, and must, be a key player in teaching real-world skills to the students around you.

Consider this: regardless of your role, perhaps the greatest impact you'll have on kids has nothing to do with academics and more to do with building skills beyond that. Since not all children have a strong connection to a teacher each year, it's on YOU.

Here's a story from my time as an elementary school principal to emphasize that point.

Realizing the necessity of every child having at least one "go-to" adult at school who knows them and cares deeply for them, especially those who were struggling at school or home for various reasons, we created a program called "Big Buddy, Little Learner." We asked elementary classroom teachers to identify any students who they had in their classroom who they believed would benefit from having an additional staff member develop a friendship with them beyond what the classroom teacher could do.

Someone who could make them feel special and build their confidence. Someone who could build up their skills necessary to be successful in life. Classroom teachers, I know what you're thinking . . . "That's me, as the classroom teacher. I already do that!" True, however, you're greatly outnumbered! And, it's next to impossible to develop that tight bond with every single one of them! And, once again, they're everywhere!

Annually, about fifteen to twenty Little Learners were identified. "Big Buddies," any staff member who volunteered, were assigned one "Little Learner." Approximately once per week, for the entire school year, the Big Buddy went out of their way to connect with the Little Learner. Big Buddies would do things like recognize great things the student did in the classroom, leave notes of encouragement in their Little Learner's locker, have lunch with them and play a board game with them during recess. They would also do things like intentionally pass them in the hall to ask them how their day was going, be the child's "go to" person to talk with, check in on, and assist with homework completion, and so on.

This was all in an attempt to recognize the student as a person, to build up their confidence and character with things "bigger" than the required curriculum. Recognizing the child, not just the student, through this program helped that child realize that someone was watching out for them at school, and they knew that we cared about their overall development, not just their academic growth. And, as for the Big Buddies, they loved it so much they kept coming back for more each year!

In this subsection, we've addressed many of the real-world skills that Character-Builders focus on in their work for students. Skills like communication, listening ("*Wait, what?*" . . . *I said listening*), collaboration, respect, responsibility, and kindness are all skills that are necessary in the real world. And, yet, they are not a part of the vast majority of curriculums. So, as an educator, ask yourself: Is the content that I teach more important than these and so many other real-world skills that the Character-Builder builds? You may not like the answer.

## FUTURE OVER PRESENT

Character-Builders recognize and embrace the influence they have on their students as people. They know that the skills they help them develop beyond the textbook or curriculum can create the person they will ultimately become. They are looking long term, far past next month, the end of the year, or even high school graduation.

Character-Builders know that they may never directly realize the impact that they've made on others. Still, they rest easy, certain that their efforts help develop good people in the long run. They, and all of us, want a future that is better than the present, either for the kids we work with or for our own kids, or both.

What separates Character-Builders from the rest of us is that instead of nodding in agreement with this statement and then going about their work for the day, they see *this* as the work. Each day they keep that focus on the future front and center, running parallel with the content that they teach (if you're not a teacher, think about what you do to get kids ready for the future beyond what you are paid to do per your assigned job duty).

> Every day I strive to get students to love school like I did. I want them to be excited about learning and I strive to be a positive role model in their lives. (Tami, elementary teacher)

**Character-Builders play chess, not checkers.** Before we offend all of you checkers players out there, read on. There's nothing wrong with playing checkers, but consider chess playing as it relates to focusing on the future over the present. Checkers players are most often engaged in thoughts and actions (moving their checkers) that are in the present. They're focused on what move they are making right now, and what their partner might do on their next move. In contrast, the chess players tend to think about moves they'll make several turns from now, and what they're opponents next several turns could be, even as they are presently making a move on the board. They are thinking into the future, like Character-Builders do. So, do you play checkers or chess?

This example of Character-Builders as chess players and how they prepare students for life in the future connects well with a needed focus we as educators have to move the current conversation beyond discussing college and career readiness to discussing helping students become "Life Ready."

> Being Life Ready means students leave high school with the grit and perseverance to overcome barriers on their path to achieve goals. Students who are Life Ready possess the growth mindset that empowers them to approach their future with confidence, to dream big, and to achieve big. Our nation's schools provide social and emotional support and experiences to equip students with the Life Ready skills they will need for success in their future. (Schroeder, 2017)

The scope of Life Readiness is defined further in the national initiative by American Association of School Administrators (AASA; the School Superintendents Association) of "Redefining Ready." The authors of this book simply refer to one quote from Schroeder's work as it connects to our point. **Character-Builders focus on preparing kids for life, not just college or careers**. Do you?

Let's dive further in with a story of why we believe a Character-Builder focuses on the future as much or more as the present. From reading thus far, we know that a strength of any school is the ability to prepare students for life by building strong character. When I left the comprehensive high school setting as a school counselor to become the principal at an alternative education high school, I quickly realized that the alternative high school was far more advanced on practices involving character development than I thought possible.

I was so impressed that the school was so intentional in its focus on this. I was also pleased to see that it was part of their identity and that they didn't shy away from letting others know that they did things differently and that this was important to them. (*I use the word "differently" on purpose as alternative education schools are often looked at as less than, rather than just different. Good alternative education schools do things differently. If they didn't, they'd get the same results as the traditional school that the students were previously unsuccessful at. Makes sense, right?*)

Anyways, one of the first things I did as the school's principal was to use my fresh perspective to recognize the powerful and different things that the school was successful at, and highlight them. It was an invigorating thing, I believe, for the staff there to have someone come in from the traditional high school setting and quickly identify the things that set them apart as educators and as a school. Their initial apprehension from having this "outsider" come into their school turned into comfort as they realized that my core values in education were aligned with theirs, to help educate students into quality people not only for today but also for the future. You see, I was thinking about the future, I was playing chess.

To "make it official," I took the well-known and often-adopted "College and Career Ready" (CCR) mantra to another level. I added another "C." Our new "C" stood for "Character." It was an official act to accentuate the commitment that we were making to teaching our students how to be good people, with strong character. I always felt proud announcing to guests or other stakeholders that we focused on CCCR skills. And, I still do.

Rewinding back a few paragraphs, we asked: Do you focus on preparing kids for life, not just college or careers? The authors of this book, a teacher and a principal, would admit that it takes work to stay focused on the future in the midst of the day-to-day craziness of our jobs. It's easy to get lost in the details each day, to play checkers instead of chess, with so much going on around us in schools every day. We're hopeful that this subsection as well as this entire CORE chapter of Character-Builder reminds you (and us) of the importance of creating better people through our work with kids each day.

Now get out there and go play some chess. Checkmate!

## SUMMARY

Character-Builders move beyond academics to focus on the whole child and creating better people. We began this chapter with a quote from someone named "Unknown," which is a strange name, but this someone must have been very wise because we see them quoted all the time! The quote ended like this, "Watch your character; it becomes your destiny." We believe that educators strong in the Character-Builder CORE shape the destiny of the students they serve because they:

- Have a whole child view
- Focus on character development
- Teach real-world skills
- Focus on the future over the present.

Character-Builders recognize the importance of spending a lot of time on relationship-building and classroom/school environments before diving too far into content. As teachers, they aren't light on content; they just know the foundational pieces of relationship-building and trust that need to be solidified before attempting the academic part of "doing school." As educators across all roles, they focus on the growth and development of the whole child.

Character-Builders prepare students by teaching them skills beyond the core curriculum and more toward skills that will be applicable for them in the real world. They know that, when students understand the content, as well as have strong character, they are more likely to be successful in life. They focus on their students as people, not just learners. They believe that those people will create a world that is better tomorrow than it is today. They believe that their calling, what's at their CORE, is preparing kids for the future, preparing chess players. They model that by being chess players each day for their students.

Said one final way, Character-Builders stand far enough back from the trees to be able to see the forest. As a result, they can see the "big picture" of their work for students. Their work each day focuses on creating people who will positively impact the world, in part because of their influence. As we've said earlier in this book, it's ok if you don't believe that you're especially strong in the Character-Builder CORE. Not everyone is. However, while reading this chapter, have you put a plan in place for something you could do tomorrow just to try it on for size?

## Perspective-Taking Scenario

Your high school math department teaching colleague seems to be hyper-focused on what appears to you to be nonacademic-related activities for her students. For example, the required geometry curriculum clearly states that the students must have an understanding of the attributes and relationships of geometric objects and that symmetry should be understood from the perspective of geometric transformation. (We may have made all that up, but unless you're a high school math teacher, you'll likely never know. So, let's move on, shall we?) Your school also has a goal of creating more respectful citizens who can help your local community and the world. To be completely honest, you've struggled over the years implementing any school-wide character-building goals and have essentially stopped trying. There's too much curriculum to teach, and not enough time to teach it.

Your colleague is attempting to accomplish teaching the required curriculum as well as honoring the character-building goal, and is having the students use reflective symmetry (using mirrors) to form perfect circles with chairs. Once the perfect circles are created with the chairs, the students will then sit in them to brainstorm ideas for the character-building goal as far as what they could do this semester during their geometry class to make the student body more respectful of one another. Your math period lasts fifty-three minutes. In your twenty-seven years of teaching, you've never been able to cover the required curriculum for the semester so that the students are prepared for their next math class. Last year, you took the math department chair position. What do you do?

## CORE Questions to Consider

1. What in your role in education could you argue is more important than helping to build kids' character which will help them be better people and create a better world?
2. Assign a percentage to what you think is more important: teaching the required curriculum OR building up a students' character? Note: You must select one and attach an unequal percentage of importance (not 50/50) to each.
3. True or False: Integrating more character-building lessons into your class can't possibly impact overall test results because there are no questions on the tests that assess character-building.

## We Dare You Challenge

For just one lesson, integrate or explicitly teach a component of character-building. Think of something "bigger" than your curriculum that you know your students will need to be successful later in life. It could be something related to being trustworthy, respectful, caring, and so on. Have the students engage in the lesson. But, be careful, student engagement is nearly guaranteed to increase, and likely increase dramatically. Also, be careful once again, as you'll have way more fun teaching today than you did yesterday!

*\*\*\*Special note/disclaimer: If an administrator comes in to observe and later questions why you were integrating character-building into your lesson, tell them Gary and Greg told you to try it. When that doesn't work, turn around and run.*

## Now What?/Action Steps

If this is your CORE, you should use it for the following actions:

- Find and focus on the strengths of each person
- Build strong, trusting relationships
- Intentionally do things that build kids up emotionally
- Develop character education programming for your school

## Why Every Team Needs Someone with the Character-Builder CORE

- To model the importance of serving the whole child
- To possess a broad scope of students and their unique needs
- To connect content to real-world examples
- To move beyond instructing on content alone

## How Identifying People with the Character-Builder CORE Helps My School Leader

- Keeps us grounded to our real purpose = developing good people
- Models and reminds us all of the value of nonacademic components of education
- Helps students become better community members/citizens
- Often connects real life situations to the learning that occurs in class
- Leads the way with building community partnerships and authentic learning

## How Understanding the Character-Builder CORE Helps Me Understand My Colleagues

- Those focused on creating better people (nonacademic skills) are actually just approaching student learning in a different way
- Needs of all learners are revealed as engagement for some students involves real-world connections
- Getting to know the whole child will become normal operating procedure for all staff
- They recognize the connection between building confidence and building up their character

*Chapter 5*

# Collaborator

**Collaborator:** unifies and empowers others to achieve shared goals together

*Never doubt that a small group of thoughtful, committed people can change the world. Indeed, it is the only thing that ever has.*

— Margaret Meade

**What we might have said:** *"You put your legs straight, and then I'll bend mine. Um, or was it I'll put my legs straight and you'll bend yours?"*

**What we should have said:** *"Oh, mom's here, let's smile for the camera and then she can help us collaborate (we were very gifted children, capable of using that word for sure) to get this thing moving."*

**What we actually said:** *"You dummy, YOUR legs are supposed to be straight. No, YOURS ARE. Mom . . ., (insert twin name here) doesn't know how to swing."*

## PERSONAL STORY

We were around eleven years old and we were out fishing with our older brother (yes, again it was Jeff, though there's an eldest brother named Mike, who may or may not make an appearance in a later chapter) and his friend. You see, they were sixteen years old so they could drive us to a lake to rent row boats and go fishing. Oh yeah, and it was a random Tuesday in April so we were missing school. Notice I didn't use the term "skipping school." It has such a negative connotation. Most of us Generation Xers think of Ferris in the classic movie *Ferris Bueller's Day Off* who of course skipped school while principal Rooney did everything he could to catch him. We were nothing like Ferris, though, we were good kids. As far as we'd like our own kids to know, anyways.

So, Gary was with our brother and Greg was with Jeff's friend (we'll call him Tom, since that's also his name). We got to the small lake in southeastern

Wisconsin early in the morning and rented boats. All was fine for the first hour or two, but then the wind picked up. In order to stabilize the boats, "The Twins," as we've been called by many since birth and by some still today, were asked to drop the anchors in their respective boats. No big deal. We're eleven. We can handle that. What could possibly go wrong, right?

Well, the anchor in Tom's boat dropped down to the bottom of the lake and the boat stabilized. Jeff's anchor went down too, but his boat continued to blow away from the shore. How could this be, you might ask? Well, anchors only work if they are firmly attached to the boat, usually by a rope. Jeff's rope was NOT secured and so they now had an anchor sitting on the bottom of the lake and a rope with nothing on the other end. Of course, it was then, and will somehow always be, "The Twins" fault.

We decided that we needed to collaborate to fix this problem. About a hundred yards down the shore, sitting neatly and undisturbed on someone's pier, was a fifty-pound (full disclosure, not sure how heavy it was but it's our story so let's just say it was a fifty-pound) cement block. It seemed to almost beckon us to come and get it to solve our anchor problem. Now, stealing would be wrong, but certainly the owner would understand our dilemma and not miss one cement block scattered among many others, right? You know where this is going, don't you?

Jeff quickly rowed toward the pier and instructed Gary to jump out, grab the cement block, and bring it back to the boat. Being that we never questioned our brother Jeff, due to the fact that there would be dire consequences, Gary did as he was told. I guess it was collaborative. I mean, they were "working together to achieve a shared goal," as our definition describes. Just as Gary picked up the block, a loud scream came from the house on the property. *"Hey kid!! Put that back NOW!"* Gary nearly dropped the block on his foot as he jumped back into the boat. Jeff immediately began to frantically row away.

You'd think the story would end there . . . but it doesn't. I mentioned that we were eleven-year-old boys. So, part of being that age means that we tend to be on the impatient side and perhaps get bored easily. Well, while Jeff and Gary were having their little adventure, Greg continued to fish. Just as the homeowner began yelling, he had casted his lure out high, toward the pier. This is one of those moments where time slows down and everything unfolds frame by frame.

While the woman is lambasting Jeff and Gary, Greg's lure managed to hit and then hook into . . . that . . . same . . . pier! This forced Tom and Greg to have to row in and unhook it. By that time, the woman had walked down from her home onto the pier. Being that she was physically so close to us, you'd think that she would have lowered her voice to a normal conversational tone. Yeah, that was not the case. She continued to scream at us. To make it worse, we weren't even the ones that tried to steal her cement block! Gary, the "Golden Child" strikes again.

As Tom and Greg got unhooked and were finally rowing away (Jeff and Gary were nearly out of sight by this time and undoubtedly laughing at us), she had to get in one last jab since she must have known that we were all together as there were no other boats out on the lake at that time.

And here it is. She said, *"Shouldn't you be in school? What kind of parents do you have that allow you to skip school and go around trying to steal people's property?"* Well, Greg was not particularly known for having a filter, but for whatever reason, he had one that day and chose to conclude that her questions were rhetorical in nature and rowed away in silence.

So, what is the lesson to be learned here? Is it, *"Don't go fishing on a windy day."* No. Or, *"Check that the anchor rope is indeed tied to the anchor before you launch it overboard."* Hard no. The real lesson learned here is one that "The Twins" still apply today: *If you lose your boat anchor while fishing, steal one.* And, now for the actual lesson: *If you have important work to get done as an educator, working alongside others will increase the likelihood of success.*

Perhaps the lesson would be more meaningful had we successfully got the cement brick, or perhaps that would have led to a lifetime of thievery and eventual prison time (though we'd have a ton more time to write a book in there, I guess). Maybe skipping, I mean missing, school was ok just this once for this valuable life lesson on the power of collaboration.

## COLLABORATOR DEFINED

"Of all the complex tasks facing educators today, none is as demanding or as critical as creating a school culture of collaboration because it is a foundation of collaboration that enables all the other work of educators to be successful. To accomplish this goal, each person who works in schools must have the disposition, knowledge, and skills to collaborate" (Friend & Cook, 2017).

This pretty much says it all. In fact, if we had a microphone to drop (if people still even do that in 2020), we'd do so here and move on to the next chapter. However, since you've already invested some of your time and money in this book, we think you deserve more. Here goes.

In regards to a CORE, we define a Collaborator as someone who *"unifies and empowers others to achieve shared goals together."* **Collaborators are leaders, with or without the formal title.** Collaborators can be absolutely anyone on your school staff. For Collaborators, it's not about them. It's about everyone else.

Whatever the end goal, Collaborators seek to achieve one thing: reaching the desired result via a sense of buy-in and ownership from all stakeholders.

After all, the group itself drives the boat (yes, a reference to our personal story shared above). Disclaimer: when we say "drive the boat," we don't mean driving an actual boat to a pier to permanently borrow (a.k.a. steal) a cement block from an unsuspecting homeowner to replace the anchor that you lost. Let's get serious again.

Collaborators, like good leaders, know that if it goes well, you praise the group. And if it flops, you take full responsibility. In administration, we call this, *"Taking none of the responsibility when things go right, and all of it when things go wrong."* So, Collaborators are all about owning the work, getting results by working together, and giving credit where credit is due.

Collaborators are also patient. They have to be. Think about it, how many impatient collaborators do you know? It takes a lot longer to hand over an issue to a group as compared to simply solving it on your own.

**Collaborators have to trust the process and accept the results**. This comes easier for some. A lot of this level of comfort has to do with the person's demeanor including their willingness and ability to "let it go." Be honest, did you just read those last three words as if you were singing them from the movie "Frozen?" Yes, yes, you did. It's ok.

We believe that the CORE of the Collaborator can best be further defined by breaking our definition down into four main subcategories as outlined below:

- Facilitator
- Assesses the Strengths of Others
- Accomplishes More TOGETHER
- Not in it for Recognition

In case you're wondering how Collaborator got to be one of the ten COREs, answer this question: *"When is the last time as an educator you spent a significant amount of time actually being completely alone?"* Wonder no more. Insert second microphone drop here.

## FACILITATOR

Here's some "good news." Collaborators don't have to be experts at everything . . . or maybe even anything! Whew. That's a relief, right? **Collaborators facilitate the work; they don't necessarily direct it or have to know everything about it**. Sounds easy, right? Well, we'd argue that there is a real art to being an effective Collaborator. If it were that easy, more people would utilize the skill of facilitation to effectively collaborate. After all, it takes great skill and knowledge to know when to jump in and when not to, what to say and what not to, who to pull in and who not to . . . to get to decisions that are best for kids.

So, if Collaborators aren't experts at everything (or anything), then how does the group achieve their goals and reach the best decisions? The quick and easy answer is that it's a collective effort. Fullan says, "The outcome, as we have seen time and time again in our own work, is that purposeful collaboration continuously contributes two interrelated powerful change forces—knowledge of ideas and practices, and identity or allegiance to one's peers and the organization" (2011). The Collaborator is very aware of these two change forces. They understand that **collaboration increases the individual knowledge of each person, but more importantly the collective knowledge of the group**. Additionally, collaborators realize that effective collaboration builds bridges between those who are collaborating (allegiance to one's peers), connecting them not only toward the particular project/goal they are working on in that moment but, more importantly, how much they overall value and enjoy working collectively with one another.

Collaborators understand that the power lies in the interrelated, always moving, parts of the group. As facilitators, they know this and refuse to take over. They know that taking control of the group could stifle creativity and progress, not to mention cause members to settle into a submissive, complacent role. The act of refusing to take over can be difficult for some, especially when they perceive that movement toward the goal is actually heading in the wrong direction.

Effective Collaborators stay silent, bite their tongue, and allow the process to play out by empowering others to contribute. They understand that the collective "will of the group" will most likely produce the best end product or decision, and one that will maximize buy-in now and in the future.

Collaborators facilitate the process by keeping it moving forward, often with short, subtle statements or thoughtful and carefully placed questions. For example, they'll use a key tactic of my mother-in-law and make statements in the form of a question. Like, *"So, are you planning to set up the playhouse that I bought for my grandchildren tomorrow then?"* You know, the kind of question that only has one right answer . . . Perhaps in an educational setting, an example might sound more like this when a principal is talking to a teacher about sharing a new instructional technique that is working well, *"Would you like to share this out at the staff meeting next week or the following one?"* You can't say "no," can you?

Additionally, **Collaborators do far more listening than speaking**. One highly regarded professional in education reminds us of this with a very thought-provoking quote about this very topic. His name is Vanilla Ice. He was a rapper in the early 1990s. In his song "Ice, Ice Baby," he states, "Stop, collaborate and **listen . . .**" You know the rest of the words and are reciting them now, aren't you? Perhaps he should have been a teacher? He's certainly strong in the Collaborator CORE. For some of you, you'll have to Google the song to listen to this portion of it. For all of you, you'll spend the rest of the day trying to get the song out of your head. You're welcome.

Educator: In meetings, are you an educator who, if you're being honest, might talk too much? Or, are you the one that stays silent? If you say too much, try listening more and learning from others in the group. If you are too quiet, speak up and share your thoughts with the team. The true value of collaboration is the sum of all the parts. "Sharing the air" isn't just for our students.

Leader: If you're a leader who likes to have their hands in everything, sit in on a committee meeting and don't say a word. Not a single word. Listen. See where the group goes without your direction. For you, collaboration might mean at times staying out of the way and letting others work together.

Another way to describe how good Collaborators facilitate positive change is to say that they, when possible, **lead more from the side rather than from the front.** Teachers often talk about the power of proximity in regards to basic tactics in preventing and responding to student behavior issues. We are also all quite familiar with a typical staff meeting where the building principal stands in front of the room to lead a meeting. This decision to physically stand front and center sends a message to the receiver.

The message, intentionally or not, is: I'm in charge and you will listen to me. While there is of course a time and place for this, it should be used less frequently than it probably is in many schools.

Collaborators deliberately avoid these power moves whenever possible and intentionally place themselves within the group. I conduct our staff meetings in a circle and select a different seat every meeting to send the message that there is no dictator in the meeting. We are seated in a formation that allows everyone to look each other in the eyes and that no one person is in any seat of power. Oftentimes, when appropriate and beneficial to the group and situation, Collaborators gently and subtly lead from the side.

Another important skill of the Collaborator as a facilitator is their **ability to keep everyone equally involved**. While this can be challenging, especially in a larger group setting, it is possible. The facilitator has the initiative and assertiveness to jump in and redirect the course of the discussion when needed. They develop the skill to be able to swoop in and ask a poignant question or make a strategic comment to get all group members back involved. Part of this comes with the ability to assess and recognize the strengths that each team member brings and how to tap into that at the right time (which we will discuss more in the next section).

The facilitator part of the Collaborator knows to say, "*Jane, you've had some very valuable experience on this topic that I know would be beneficial for the group to hear about.*" Facilitators keep the work moving in the right direction by keeping all members involved and contributing to the conversation.

> I am supposed to be with kids. To teach, to give, to share and to learn from them. I know that, together, we can do great things. (CK, elementary teacher)

## ASSESSES THE STRENGTHS OF OTHERS

Collaborators achieve positive results in part because of the talents, skills, and abilities of those around them. However, the key is their ability to **recognize and leverage these talents, skills, and abilities in others which helps to obtain the desired results**. Collaborators possess this skill, probably partially innate and partially learned, and use it to place the right people "on the bus" and to get them "in the right seats." What we mean by this specific to this portion of the chapter is that they know which educators to have on certain teams and when to lean on them for their expertise.

The act of placing the right people in the right places results in an empowering feeling for those members. They are in places where they are passionate, skilled, accomplished, and strong. They feel confident that they can offer something to the team. And, putting the right people in the right places by assessing their strengths isn't just for adults.

Teachers, think about your students. What strengths do each of them possess? From one teacher to another, if we're being honest, you admittedly may have to dig a little deeper for some. But they're there. And, they're abundant. Now, how could you use those strengths within every student to make for a better experience for them, and for your class? And, regardless of your role in education, pause to ponder how you are assessing the strengths of others, and how you are leveraging those strengths to do great things for kids.

**Collaborators guide others to fully utilize their talents for the good of the group**. They focus on one, most important thing: getting the best results for students. I believe that Williams and Hierck were talking about any educator taking the lead when they wrote, "High-performing leaders know that they cannot get results by themselves or expect to own all the best ideas. A leader is only as good as the strengths of the people around him or her, so effective leaders surround themselves with those who can strongly contribute to both guiding coalitions and collaborative teams" (2015). Collaborators ability to assess the strengths of those around them is critical to creating a highly effective team. That highly effective team, then, can do great things for students, more than any one person could do individually.

Educator: Think of a student who you work with who often struggles. List 3-5 of their strengths. Now assess yourself: *Do you put this student in a place to best utilize those strengths?* If not, change YOU, not them.

Leader: Since the most effective leaders surround themselves with people fully utilizing their own strengths, ask yourself: *How do I know I've placed team members in the right places (grade, course, duty, etc.)?* (Hint: make sure you know everyone's CORE).

As a first year Assistant Superintendent, I knew there was a lot I didn't know. It was obvious to me that I had some gaps that needed to be filled and my first thought was of my principal colleagues who I now supervised. One such gap I identified was in my new role in leading the Educator Effectiveness (EE) component (at the time, the new staff evaluation process) for our district. For those of you who aren't familiar, Wisconsin defines EE as a "performance-based continuous improvement system designed to improve the education of all students in the state of Wisconsin by supporting guided, individualized, self-determined professional growth and development of educators." Yeah, great. Now I'm leading it!

I knew going into that year, even as a former principal, that there were other principals more knowledgeable than I was about EE. And yet, I was charged with leading them through what would essentially be year two of implementation of this process. This meant ensuring that all administrators went through and passed the rigorous training process required to be able to complete staff evaluations that year. And, with this newer model that the state had recently adopted, ensure smooth implementation and communication for teachers of this evaluation system as more came up on their Summary (evaluation cycle) year. Insert stomachache and sleepless nights here.

We define a Collaborator as someone who empowers others while facilitating the work. Along that line of thinking, I created a team of several building principals at the elementary level, both middle schools, two associate principals from the high school and two other district office leaders to aide in this process. So, how did I lead through a collaborative model? We had a running Google document throughout the year, where we asked and answered each other's questions. Then communicated this information out to other building leaders. We met at least once each month to further discuss the questions as well as other topics related to EE.

These administrators were also charged with informing their administrative colleagues at their school level of our conversations. Additionally, I created a teacher EE team, with representatives of several educators from each level, to check in on actual implementation in their schools and bring classroom examples of how the process was going. We met throughout the year as well, with their input being invaluable.

This story is a great example of how any educator can first assess and then leverage others strengths to work together toward a common goal. In this story, collaboratively, we not only survived EE (well, maybe I did, with the help of some Tums), but thrived in it!

## ACCOMPLISHES MORE TOGETHER

> *Many hands make light work.*
>
> —John Heywood

We want to start this section of the chapter with this quote because it's a main component of being a Collaborator. Along with Collaborators being strong facilitators and assessing group members strengths, **they also understand that more and better work is accomplished TOGETHER**. This starts with the assessment of personal strengths as discussed in the previous section. Then, collaborators take these strengths and recognize that putting them together will result in a much stronger end product.

The Collaborator knows and is committed to this philosophy of working together. They also realize that one of the positive results is people feeling connected to and responsible for one another.

> The power of collective capacity is that it enables ordinary people to accomplish extraordinary things—for two reasons. One is that knowledge about effective practice becomes more widely available and accessible on a daily basis. The second reason is more powerful still—working together generates commitment. (Fullan, 2015)

This accomplishes a very important part of the success of any group: its members feeling that they are needed and have something to offer. **Collaborators know that higher quality work can be accomplished TOGETHER and that it builds a sense of worth in its team members**. That sense of worth creates a culture in the school that impacts decisions made today as well as in the future because staff members understand that they as an individual are an important part of the "together" that we're discussing in this part of the chapter.

The Collaborator realizes (and eventually counts on) the team making significant progress toward the goal because TOGETHER they want to, not necessarily for the approval of the administrator. Fullan wrote, "The goal of having a collaborative culture is not that employees will do the work for a resolute leader, but rather that they become collectively engaged in work that is meaningful to them" (2011).

A perfect example of this is a sign that has been hanging in my office for many years and it reminds me about the importance of staff buy-in. Picture a landscape-formatted poster with a horizontal line equally separating the page in half. Above the line is the word "Commitment," and below the line is the word "Compliance." Its basic interpretation is that you always want COMMITMENT OVER COMPLIANCE. So true. And, moreover, that's only accomplished by working *together*.

> "*Together*" is the key word in my story. We all experience "differing abilities" throughout our lifetime. It's actually how we learn to accept and cope with the challenges and successes of our differences that builds our character! Being a part of a team where all members work "together" and learn from one another is the best success story of them all! (Yvette, elementary teacher)

The last component of a strong Collaborator's commitment to the concept of accomplishing more together involves building bridges. Collaborators take people with a wide variety of talents (not to mention personalities, or did we just mention that by saying we weren't going to mention it?) and get them to work well together.

Think about all the different personalities in your grade, no . . . in the teaching staff, no . . . in the entire staff. Getting them to more often see their similarities as educators, while believing that their differences are strengths, not hurdles, is what the Collaborator does. This concept holds true for the students you work with as well.

**Collaborators artfully connect those with differing skill sets and facilitate their work together.** These folks probably don't even realize what is happening because they are so caught up in the powerful work that is being done. It's human nature to get caught up in things when we enjoy them (even work!). Time flies when you're having fun, right? Collaborators look for commonalities that people bring to the table, and provide a bridge of sorts between them. They look for what educators can all agree on and build from there. They then help those educators work together to ensure safe passage across said bridge to get to the best destinations for kids. **Collaborators accomplish more together.** Period. (Or, did we not have to say "Period" because there was one?)

## NOT IN IT FOR RECOGNITION

Abraham Lincoln once said, "Don't worry when you are not recognized, but strive to be worthy of recognition." (Note to self: When writing a book, if you're going to quote a president, make it one who is ranked in the top 3 by most historians.)

Collaborators couldn't care less about being acknowledged for their successes. They are not motivated to be recognized for their achievements. Not only do Collaborators not desire recognition, they are known to deflect any attention that may come their way to others around them. They'd prefer to simply conduct their powerful work, so focused on the work that recognition for it isn't even on their radar. When recognition does come their way, you'll typically find them looking at their shoes. Think about it, as an educator, for everything that you do for kids every day, for how much of it are you officially "recognized" for? Likely, not much. But, do you really care? Likely not. Good for you! That's not why you do what you do. You're humble. Perhaps so much so that Collaborator is at your CORE. Well?

So, we know that Collaborators aren't in it for the recognition when things are going well. Connected to that, the question that as educators we now face more and more is about improving academic results of the students we serve. Specific to this section of the book, the natural question then is: *"Does collaboration among teachers, administration and parents increase test scores?"*

Also, we know that **collaboration increases trust among stakeholders**. So, the next logical question is: *"Does that increase in trust equate to an increase in student achievement?"* Here's the answer: "The most effective schools, based on test score improvement over time after controlling for demographic factors, had developed an unusually high degree of 'relational trust' among their administrators, teachers, and parents" (Anrig, 2015). So there you have it, an increase in trust can, as supported by research, equate to an increase in test scores. Is a third microphone drop in one chapter too much? We think not.

Educator: How could you infuse collaboration tomorrow for your students? Take that whole class lesson, recess duty, small group time, etc. and find a way to inject collaboration. The lessons they'll learn might be far bigger than the content!

Leader: You don't have to do it all yourself. Select a larger task you've typically completed by yourself and try to include others this time around. The end result will likely be better with collaboration!

I learned an important lesson about collaboration in my first year as department chairperson of the student services department in a comprehensive high school. The entire department noticed a disconnect between us and the rest of the staff, mostly the teachers. The lack of knowledge or understanding (perspective-taking) about the role of specialists in schools is common. And, if we're being honest, perhaps we weren't understanding their perspective from the teacher point of view as well. The work of student services personnel is heavy on individual, confidential services. This results in many staff not really knowing "what those people down in their office do all day."

So our department set out to do a better job of communicating what we were doing on our part to support students. While the details of the changes are too numerous to mention, overall, we just tried to dispel the "old school" ideas that many staff had about what we did.

Students were released at 3:00 p.m. every day, and the staff day ended soon after. I thought that it'd be great to offer voluntary, informal collaboration time to any staff person who wanted to come speak with us about any student or any situation. What better time than when the day is done. So, knowing that nearly every student service person worked late every day, I came up with a GREAT idea (at least, in my mind).

As department chairperson, I would make it clear to all staff that a student services person would be available after school every day until at least 4:00 p.m. I proudly called it, "Open Door Till 4 (o'clock) . . . Or More." Catchy right? We all worked until 4:30 p.m.–5:00 p.m. most days anyways, and so no matter who came down to talk with us, one of us would be there. Even if the rest of the team needed or wanted to leave earlier than normal, it didn't matter. I would cover it and update the school counselor the next day.

Well, I was ready the next Tuesday morning for our all staff meeting. The library began to fill up for our weekly 7:05 a.m. staff meeting. As each of the ninety or so staff people came in and took a seat, I became more excited. After covering what he needed to cover, the principal handed the floor over to me. I stood up and turned toward my peers to talk. I energetically shared the plan for the "Open Door Till 4 . . . Or More" with the staff. Crickets. No response. Now, I hadn't expected a standing ovation, but maybe a head nod or an eyebrow raise (or at least a fake smile) would have been nice.

Well, it actually wouldn't be fair to say that there was no reaction. As I glanced over at the table where my school counselor colleagues were sitting, there was definitely a reaction. Their eyes were wide open, eyebrows raised, and mouths were hung open, just enough to express their disbelief. I had failed to communicate this plan with them. I had failed to *collaborate*. They likely believed I was doing this not only for us as counselors to be available for staff but also for the recognition. Their reaction was a range of discomfort to anger. Message received.

I learned that day that when working with teams, sometimes it doesn't really matter how good your idea is. Instead, it's all about the collaborative process. **It's about working *together* on a good idea to make it even better.** And, most importantly, connected to this part of the chapter, it's about the quality of the end product, not the recognition for it. I'm happy to say that this was the first and last time (as far as you know) that I so miserably failed to collaborate. I learned my lesson, and am hopeful that my lesson transfers to your work so that you can avoid a similar situation entirely!

## SUMMARY

We define a person who is strong in the Collaborator CORE as someone who "unifies and empowers others to achieve shared goals together." We believe that those Collaborators in the school where you work each day have the following four characteristics in common:

- Facilitator
- Assesses the Strengths of Others
- Accomplish More TOGETHER
- Not in it for Recognition

A quote we used early on in this chapter and one that bears repeating is that it is the "foundation of collaboration that enables all the other work of educators to be successful" (Friend & Cook, 2017). We asked you to think about that for a moment and answer this question specific to your role in your school: *What work do you do that is done alone, with no input, influence, or interaction with others?* Your answer might very well be, *"None."* Or, it might be, *"Not very much, and that work is not my favorite part of the job."* Collaboration is all around you, yet something before reading this chapter that you may not have yet fully appreciated its prevalence and power.

While of course we hope you made frequent use of your highlighter or pen as you marked up the chapter as you read, you may be one of those people who either prefers not to mark up a book (because your mom told you never to write in books) or prefers to read without stopping to take written notes. Either way, this summary is for you as we've bulleted some of the best (or at least what we believe are the best) statements from the chapter.

- Collaboration increases the individual knowledge of each person and, more importantly, the collective knowledge of the group, to achieve goals.
- For Collaborators, it's not about them. It's about everyone else.
- Collaborators let go of their power and put trust in others.
- Effective collaboration builds bridges between those who are collaborating.
- Collaborators are generally humble enough to recognize when others may have what's needed and don't hesitate to incorporate them in order to achieve results.
- Collaborators get their fulfillment from achieving goals together.
- Collaborators couldn't care less about the recognition.

We hope that reviewing these most powerful statements serves as a reminder for you to leverage that part inside you to better utilize your skills of collaboration. We also hope it reminds you to think about how you can assist your team, administrator, or school if you are strong in the Collaborator CORE and you see areas of the school that bringing staff together could help make your service better for kids. Finally, we hope that reading this chapter helped you gain perspective for other educators in your school who may be especially strong in this CORE. Let's put that to the test right now in the Perspective-Taking Scenario section below. Good luck.

## Perspective-Taking Scenario

Consider this quote from Fullan's Change Leader: "From the perspective of the change leader, collaboration means that the circle of leadership should always be expanding to incorporate the meaning and motivation of the full group" (p. 108).

This school year there is a new committee being formed which will focus on building up the school culture. The principal stated in the first staff meeting of the year that she wants to come up with some ideas to make the school a more positive place to be for both staff and students. While she has some ideas, she's looking to form a team consisting of one staff member per grade level or department for a "Culture Club" (think of the 1980s band with Boy George—some of you youngsters won't have a clue).

You are already too busy, and not necessarily looking for "one more thing." Your colleague approaches you and says *"I'll Tumble 4 Ya"* (again, need that Boy George background info here) if you sign up for this committee and follows with *"Do You Really Want to Hurt Me"* (another one) by making ME sign up for yet another committee? Almost unbelievably, she closes with, it's bad *"Karma Chameleon"* (another) to sign up for this committee because it will *"Come and go, come and go"* (ok, last one) like everything else in education. What do you say to her (bonus points for using a Culture Club lyric)?

## CORE Questions to Consider

1. Why are Collaborators critical to the success of every school?
2. How has collaboration increased student achievement in your school? Or, has it at all?
3. Think of your favorite boss/leader of all time. Was he/she a Collaborator? What, if anything, does that tell you about the power of collaboration?

## We Dare You Challenge

# 1:
Think of an upcoming unit/project/task that you have on your plate. I dare you to approach a colleague in your department/grade/work group that you don't typically work with and make time to collaborate around the issue. The results will likely blow your mind (and perhaps even save you time along the way)!
# 2:
I dare you to use a Culture Club lyric at your next staff meeting. (If this makes no sense to you, then you skipped reading the scenario above. If you skipped reading the scenario and it still makes sense to you, then you might want to make an appointment with your doctor.)

## Now What?/Action Steps

If this is your CORE, you should use it for the following actions:

- To think, "Who can add value to this issue?" instead of, "How will I solve this myself?"
- Be a better listener than a talker
- Model it by actively engaging self and others in meetings and conversations
- Ask questions and prompt people who you know have a lot to offer, but may not typically feel comfortable offering it
- Take none of the credit as an individual, rather give the credit to others

Why Every Team Needs Someone with the Collaborator CORE

- TEAM (Together Everyone Achieves More)
- To have fun working with people who acknowledge everyone's collective efforts

- To have trust in them because they have felt included and part of the process before
- To work with people who are humble and not interested in recognition

How Identifying People with the Collaborator CORE Helps My School Leader

- The best solutions come from utilizing the expertise and experiences of others
- Builds bridges around commonalities
- The collaborative environment leads to things feeling related and more manageable
- Creates a culture of equity among staff, regardless of role
- Removes the pressure from a leader to be an expert on everything

How Understanding the Collaborator CORE Helps Me Understand My Colleagues

- Sees the power of working toward the same goals as a team
- Speaking up and sharing ideas result in the best solutions
- Some people process things better out loud and with others
- Being vocal does not equal being difficult
- Are passionate about getting it done right, not just getting it done

*Chapter 6*

# Connector

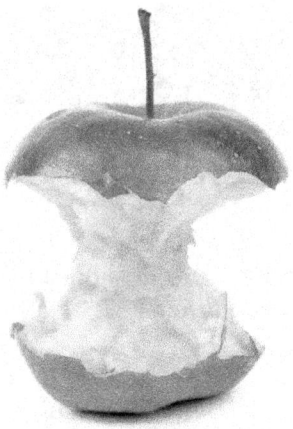

**Connector:** understands and is committed to the strength of relationships.

*I've learned that people will forget what you said, people will forget what you did, but people will never forget how you made them feel.*

—Maya Angelou

**"Hey, twin brother, are you wringing my neck or hugging me? We've got the weirdest relationship. I'm just not connecting with your signals. I know you care, but this is a little much."**

## PERSONAL STORY

So, it's fairly obvious that a Connector is all about relationships—making connections with others (we're not rocket scientists, after all). Growing up, one of our brothers thought that it was his life's mission to "create" relationships for us, his younger, twin brothers. This will make more sense in a minute. And, upon further reflection, it was not as much about helping us gain relationships with others as much as it was about embarrassing us whenever humanly possible. Allow us to explain.

So, when the middle child (yes, it's Jeff again) of a family of four boys was sixteen and old enough to drive, he was ready to now integrate his ability to use the car into his already impressive resume of ways to embarrass us. One important point to understand is that having all four of your boys involved in numerous sports activities equated to A LOT of driving around.

So, when Jeff was old enough to drive, he was "voluntold" to drive us to and from our practices and games. Well, in 1985 Jeff was sixteen and we were eleven. Now, eleven years old is a prime age to be easily and thoroughly embarrassed, especially with the opposite sex. Jeff knew this and had MANY strategies to accomplish his mission. We'll share only one in this story. We didn't know it then, but he was, and still is, very strong in the Connector CORE.

One such technique occurred on multiple occasions while he was driving us around in mom's 1977 Ford Fairmont. He would see a girl around our age outside of their house or riding their bike and he would instinctively know when we knew them (ok, maybe he just noticed us slipping down in our vinyl seat to hide). Anyway, he would slowly drive up to them so they were on the passenger side where we were seated. He would then yell out, *"Hey, my brother thinks you're cute,"* or *"My brother likes you."* We would get incredibly embarrassed as evidenced by our beet red faces as he would squeal away with a smirk on his face and a snicker.

What's more, just when we thought we could forget the awful experience, we would go to school the next day and be confronted by the girls he had yelled at. We'd have to either avoid them altogether or approach them and tell them that our brother does that all the time to us. Since we were eleven and couldn't talk to girls, we typically chose the former. It's no wonder that we had trouble talking to girls as we entered our teen years. Thanks a lot, Jeff. Being embarrassed, and then forced to constantly relive it, was the gift from Jeff that kept on giving time after time. So, was he a Connector? Perhaps, but perhaps not. Either way, we tip our hat to him. Well played, Jeff. Well played.

## CONNECTOR DEFINED

In regards to a CORE, we define a Connector as someone who "understands and is committed to the strength of relationships with people." They prioritize building and maintaining relationships above all else, as a means to connect with others, feel fulfilled and accomplish goals (and in doing so, they also help others achieve the same results).

Simply put, Connectors have an innate ability to relate to other people in a way that makes them feel accepted and valued. Sounds pretty easy, right? The reality is, it's not. Good Connectors just make it look easy. **The Connector knows that in order to accomplish their own goals, they need to build and maintain strong relationships with others**. They realize that, in doing so, they're not only helping themselves, in the school setting they're more importantly helping others. Read on.

Connectors are all about relationships, and typically give much more than they receive. Saenz wrote, "Many would go so far as to argue that relationships are our most important resource—in the end, far more valuable to us than money, education, or physical ability" (2016). Educator Connectors would agree and tap into the power of building relationships as their most important and valuable resource toward helping others. They fully grasp that people require positive human interaction and connections to survive and thrive (reach goals).

In education, those connections equate to increased student achievement. Connectors get the most academically out of their kids due to having strong relationships with them. As you read this chapter, think about the Connectors in your school. What strengths do they bring to serving kids? Keep an open mind about them, even if the Connector is not one of your COREs. Doing so will help you better know their purpose, and understand their perspective.

We believe that the CORE of Connector can be further defined by breaking our definition down into four main subcategories as outlined below:

- Relationships are the Foundation
- Genuine Care for Others
- Personable and Approachable
- Trust is Earned and Valued ("Val**you**d")—We didn't invent that, but we'll take the credit if you've never heard it before! For the Connector, it is indeed all about YOU!

## RELATIONSHIPS ARE THE FOUNDATION

"Many improved practices in education that have been developed over the past two decades have been less successful than they might have been because they have focused primarily on curriculum, instruction, assessment, and modes of service delivery" (Comer, 2015). Wow, that's a powerful way to begin this section. Especially coming from a current principal, and a former principal and district office leader. After all, aren't all of "those people" supposed to be all about delivery of curriculum, instruction, and assessment to improve student achievement? If you are an administrator, don't worry, the authors are also about these things.

However, the reality is that **we see building strong relationships in schools as the very foundation necessary to get the results that all educators are working so hard for.** Think of eating an apple. The core is the center (in case you didn't know). Without the core as the foundation, there is no apple. Carrying that forward regarding Connectors . . . without relationships, there is a less solid foundation for increasing student achievement. Building relationships is at the CORE (see what we did there?—shameless plug for our own book!) When relationships are strong, then and only then can results (i.e., test data) improve for students. We're not suggesting it's the only factor, but it is at the foundation of educators getting "home" relative to student achievement.

**Connectors understand that relationships are the KEY component to get the most out of any initiative (school goal, lesson plan, improving student behavior or engagement).** Think about it. How many times have you seen a pretty darn good plan or lesson go awry early on and stay there (again, there are many potential reasons, but stay in the relationship mindset)? We like to say that the best-laid plans can fall apart when you add just one thing to it . . . people. Without committed players who are "all in" because they have a strong relationship with one another, prepare for a greater struggle than is necessary.

I have a sign in my office that reminds me of this. It says, "Culture Eats Strategy For Breakfast." That says it all. It's all about relationships. (Note that I like my culture with a side of bacon. But, don't we all?)

**Connectors invest in people, not things**. They spend a lot of time and energy on getting to know people and developing relationships. For teachers, this could equate to days at the beginning of the school year creating a classroom culture that is prepared for learning. For administrators, this means scheduling time in your day (like you'd schedule and keep a meeting with a parent or the superintendent) to connect with the very people you lead. More specifically, this means "shaking hands and kissing babies" (it's a figure of speech, if you want to keep your job) each morning if possible for ten minutes before school to say hello to staff, parents and welcome students.

Educator: Identify a student who is the most "lost." Now, commit to giving them some of your time to develop a trusting relationship. Don't allow their potential initial response of pushing you away discourage you. Pull them closer. Connect with them.

Leader: Identify a staff person who you may have not connected with yet in terms of getting to know them. Commit time to doing so. What you (both) get out of it will be well worth it.

Connectors also understand that relationships don't just maintain themselves. Ummm, sounds like something your spouse or significant other might say? They're right (but we won't tell them that). **Relationships require ongoing focus and maintenance.** The work the Connector does to help maintain strong relationships is like the oil change that your car needs every few thousand miles to keep it running efficiently. Without it, things start breaking down. If this ongoing maintenance is left undone for too long, that car may be headed to the junkyard. Not a good place for a car, or a relationship.

This focus on maintenance can be demonstrated in many ways. One example is when a Connector follows up with someone days or weeks after an initial interaction about something the other educator brought to them. They value that relationship so much that they will make time (even calendar it) to maintain and even strengthen it. These follow-ups are generally around a topic that may not be all that personally important to the Connector, but they realize the level of importance it is to the other person. **So, from the Connector's point of view, if it's important to someone else, then it's important to them.**

> I strive to build meaningful and lasting relationships with my students and their families in hopes of making the world a better place one child at a time! (Christine, special education teacher)

Connectors can at first glance seem to focus too much on relationships and not enough on goal attainment, including academics. On the contrary, **Connectors are all about results**. They just lean on relationships with people as a vehicle to attain them.

Want to get students to engage in a unit that you are starting on Monday? Not going to happen to the full extent that it could without some level of relationship with them. Want a new school program or initiative to hit the ground running? You will have had to develop some strong relationships first. Expect parents and other community members to volunteer at an exciting new activity next month? Relationships required.

It's these relationships that will, in the end, produce the positive results Connectors strive for. After all, they've got all of the oil changes, now it's time to enjoy the drive!

Here's a personal story as it connects to the Connector CORE. As a second-year teacher (about a hundred years ago), I had a first grade student (we'll call her Sarah) who had selective mutism. Admittedly, I knew nothing about this topic. So, I did what any teacher would do:

- Panicked
- Researched selective mutism (not as simple back then as "googling it" today—it's true, Google hasn't always been around; "goggle it" to fact check me if you like)
- Reached out to her parents to learn more about her including her interests

- Talked with school resource staff
- Panicked some more
- Spent extra time those first few weeks with the child
- Asked her parents to videotape her at home talking up a storm and with permission showed it to the class (with an actual video cassette—you may have to Google that too)
- Finished it all up with some more panicking

Despite my efforts, Sarah remained mute in the school setting. I was stumped. I then reviewed my notes from the meeting that I had with her parents and was reminded that Sarah loved Scooby Doo (I'm more of a Shaggy kind of a guy, but I wasn't about to hold that against her). I went to the store to buy any Scooby Doo items that I could find, including stickers, a coloring book, a notebook with Scooby on the cover, pencils, and so on.

Over the course of the next few weeks, I gave her a little gift here and there. With each gift, she smiled politely and I could tell that I was starting to connect with her. However, she hadn't talked yet. What she didn't know was that I had one final item that I had not mentioned yet: a Scooby tie. I woke up one morning sensing that she was primed for today to be the day that she finally talked in school (Insert the Dumb and Dumber movie quote here: "*So you're telling me there's a chance!*"(Google it)). As she walked into my classroom that morning, I've admittedly never since seen a child's face light up with so much excitement at my attire. Perhaps my wife is right, I need a new wardrobe. Or, perhaps Sarah and I had a breakthrough in our relationship at that moment.

Now, I'd love to say that our relationship changed in that second, that she ran over and shouted so loud with excitement that I actually wanted to tell her to be quiet (which would have been awkward . . . and awesome at the same time). However, the reality is that's not exactly what happened. Instead, later on that day, I approached her during writing time to see what she was going to write about. It's then that she whispered her first words to me . . . "*I like your tie.*" I'll never forget those four little words.

They were a sign for me, and I hope for you, that building relationships, being a Connector, takes work but pays off in the end. As you've read so far in this chapter, you've learned about the importance of building relationships with those you work with and serve, and that doing so is foundational. For Sarah, I'm not sure what I taught her that year, and she might not know either. However, over twenty years later, I bet she remembers that day as well as I do, including and most importantly that feeling she had when she talked for the first time in school. I'm hoping it was life changing for her. It was for me.

*Chapter 6*

# GENUINE CARE FOR OTHERS

**Connectors possess genuine, unconditional, positive regard for all.** The key here is the word "genuine." What makes it so powerful is that it is REAL. Not forced. Not fake. Not manufactured. Being truly genuine is a key ingredient for Connectors. When Connectors are fully engaged in a conversation with a person, they are all in, looking them in the eyes and nodding and responding to demonstrate their level of involvement.

Connectors genuinely care about what others are saying on a deeper level. They know when to listen, and when to offer advice. And, when they listen, it's the genuine (not just wait for you to stop talking so they can talk) kind of listening.

Connectors show their genuine care and concern in different ways. Since they see the strong connection between actions in school to people's lives occurring outside of it, they are often open to discuss, and at times even bring up, personal topics. For example, they know that in order to get students to reach their full academic potential, they must remove or minimize any barriers to their learning.

This is only possible by addressing issues outside of the school setting. Specific to other staff members like administrators, they know that in order to get the most out of staff, they must address and support challenges that staff face outside of their jobs. We believe, as do those strong in the Connector CORE, that educators in general have come a long way with recognizing this necessity for building connections with students.

However, we believe many educators have room for improvement as it relates to building connections with one another as fellow staff members. Doing so will help those educators better know and understand their colleagues, including why they believe what they believe and why they act the way they act. This will help with the "perspective" of others theme that continues to come up throughout this book.

Educators are people first. Connectors see that in their relationship with fellow educators. Do you?

Educator: Since educators are people first, students need to see them that way. Allow yourself to be vulnerable and let students in to some aspect of your life. Share a personal story with your students today. It will be fun for everyone, including you.

Leader: Since leaders are people first, staff need to see them that way. Allow yourself to be vulnerable and let staff into your life. Share a personal story at your next staff meeting. It will be fun for everyone, including you. Then, allow others to do the same from time to time (perhaps it would be a fun way to begin those staff meetings that everyone loves attending!)

Connectors know that, "In every classroom, relationships among individuals are either facilitating students' learning or preventing it" (Smith, Fisher & Fry, 2015). This is why teacher Connectors place so much time and energy on relationship-building, both at the beginning of the year or class and ongoing as needed. When a teacher (or any staff member) focuses on maintaining and rebuilding relationships throughout the year, their students benefit greatly. In fact, it can be considered healthy or restorative in nature.

"Restorative practices" is a term that many readers are likely familiar with and was mentioned in a previous chapter. It is based on the idea that people are far more likely to change their behaviors based on the bonds they have with others, rather than any forced sense of obligation to follow rules. Essentially, their genuine care for others helps restore relationships that have been harmed in some way. So, in the classroom setting, a punitive response like moving a clip down on a behavior chart, missing recess, or receiving a detention (while potentially impactful for some kids) does little to replace the old behavior or motivate toward a new one.

These punitive acts can even shame or shun some students from their school family (their class). Connectors know this and, in regard to restorative practices, focus on repairing relationships to their original condition to improve the chances of better results in the long term.

Smith, Fisher, and Frey go further to state, "Restorative practices build on the positive relationships that adults foster with students and with each other in schools. When students care about the relationships they have with others, they work to keep those relationships healthy and to repair any damage to them" (2015). We would submit that kids yearn for and require positive relationships more than anyone. They may not say it or show it, but they do. **So, when a student makes a poor decision or misbehaves, don't push them away, pull them closer**.

We understand that can be very tricky to do, especially when your own emotions are involved (and perhaps you're in the middle of teaching a lesson!). However, helping students restore their behavior based on your positive response will serve them (and you) well in the long run. So, instead of taking away minutes from their recess or giving them a detention, consider talking with them individually to see how you can work together moving forward.

If it helps, think of it this way: *Is taking away a 142nd recess really going to help them?* Likely not. You know the definition of insanity, right? The look on their face when you show them you genuinely care might just make their day, and it will make yours for sure! Give it a try. What do you have to lose? Sidenote: Now, when they don't have to stay in for recess, you actually have time to run to the bathroom! It's a win for everyone, including your bladder!

In my first month as the principal at an alternative education high school, I was faced with numerous student behavioral challenges. Looking back, I realize now that students were testing me to determine where the lines were. Being a school counselor previously, I brought a skill set that would no doubt help me connect with people, but it also meant that I lacked experience in responding to challenging behaviors in the way a principal or assistant principal must.

One day a student's cell phone went missing from a classroom. The student was irate that someone would steal it when it was plugged in just across the room from where they were sitting. Since he didn't realize it was gone until thirty or so minutes after the period had ended, there was little I could do besides check hallway cameras, speak with students in the class, and essentially ask around. I knew that whoever took it likely didn't have it on them anymore. Our students were raised to not get involved or "snitch" on other people (the kids say, "snitches get stitches," right?), so I knew that the chances of me retrieving the phone were slim to none.

My investigation turned up one prime suspect, "Shawn." Shawn was acting suspiciously right after and had asked multiple teachers about what would happen to the person who took it if they got caught. Shawn and I had a few interactions already that year and he was really starting to buy in (or so I thought) to the caring school environment that we were working so hard to create. Shawn was also seeing that we handled behavioral issues differently than his previous school which was a large, comprehensive high school. Being a smaller school with at-risk students, we needed to create different ways to teach, assess, and treat students.

Anyways, I called Shawn into my office and questioned him about the phone. He adamantly denied having anything to do with it. Now, Shawn had been caught stealing iPads from his previous school and selling them on the street, so I knew he was capable of doing something like this. However, as I was talking with him, I was really hoping that he saw that something like this would damage the safe, family feel of our school and impact the relationships that he was building with his classmates.

As I questioned him, however, I could sense that he was lying. My mind went to offering him a scenario where he could fix what went wrong, if he wanted to. I reminded Shawn of the intake meeting he had attended where we discussed the expectations of the school and how we are a family here. I also reiterated that like other families, our school family has issues sometimes. And, that if we were going to be a close-knit family, we needed to trust each other and make things right when we caused harm in any way. Essentially, I was showing him that I cared about him and that I wasn't going to handle the situation the way he was used to.

I told Shawn that if the phone turned up anywhere back at school, I would take that as a sign that the person who took it acted impulsively, but now wanted to do the right thing. I told him that hopefully it would be placed in my mailbox in the main office or even left somewhere that could be easily found and turned in.

Well, long story short, Shawn decided not to do any of those things. He did one better. The next school day, Shawn walked straight into my office, looked me in the eyes and handed me the phone. He was prepared to accept any and all responsibilities for his actions, even if that meant harsh consequences and police involvement. Instead, it resulted in a conversation where Shawn explained why he had taken the phone and how awful he felt about it.

He talked about how he was trying so hard to change his ways, but that he took steps backward sometimes. He shared how his family issues and living situation had pushed him to take the phone in the first place. But most importantly, he talked about how this school offered him something different and he didn't want to lose that. Essentially, he was showing his genuine care for our school family.

Shawn decided on his own to repair the harm that he created. He would apologize to the person whose phone he stole, apologize to the class in which he created an untrusting environment in, and finally, assist in creating and delivering a school-wide message about respect. Again, all on his own. Why? Because the experience meant something to him and instead of being punished, he wanted to make it right. This was a powerful life lesson about the power of RP and the power that a Connector has. Come to think of it, as much as I was a Connector for Shawn, I realize now that in the end he was as much or more a Connector for his classmates as I was for him. Powerful stuff indeed. And, now several years later, Shawn and I have not once had a similar conversation about him taking property that wasn't his. Not once. Wouldn't it be great to have our students always learn "a lesson" the first time? With connections, it's more possible than you may think.

## PERSONABLE AND APPROACHABLE

Connectors are people you want to be around. It's not just that they are positive, energetic, or passionate; it's because they are personable and approachable. They are easy to talk with about anything. They're the kind of people who draw you toward them, even if you're not normally an overly social person. You don't really know why, but your feet seem to uncontrollably move toward them when you see them (or, if you're an introvert, at least not walk away). You see it happening, and seem to have no power over it.

**Connectors are visible**. They refuse to hide away in their classroom or office, choosing instead to be out in the open with their sleeves rolled up ready to engage with others regardless of their role. This is an intentional practice and is a strategic effort to be around others as much as possible. The more visible they are, the more opportunities they have to interact with other people. The more positive interactions they have, the more positive relationships they create and maintain. The more these relationships can be transformed into improving the educational experience, the better the results for kids.

This visibility can make it feel like a Connector is everywhere. They are at the front doors at student arrival time, outside their classroom door during passing times, in the hallways, in the cafeteria, attending sporting events, at the school musical, and so on. Not only are Connectors physically present all over the place, but they also bring a positive vibe and energy with them. They typically are found with a smile on their face. They are "glass half full" people, every time you see them. How do they do that? Even on a Monday? Even before their morning cup of coffee kicks in? Read on.

**Connectors are also strong communicators**. How couldn't they be? It's part of what makes them personable and approachable. We're not sure if there could be a more important component to the Connector's repertoire. They understand one of the key components of effective communication: It doesn't matter what you meant; it matters how it was received.

So, Connectors are very aware of their word choice, along with their body language. They are skilled at reading people and adjusting their message accordingly. This allows them to know the best times to sit back or the best times to push forward in any situation. From a teacher Connector perspective, this can mean getting the most out of each student during a lesson. From a school leader Connector perspective, this can mean getting the most out of staff when deploying a new initiative because of their communication skills.

Similarly, **Connectors are able to say a lot, even when saying very little**. Note that this is significantly different from when you ask your spouse a question while watching the game on TV and s/he—likely he—grunts back at you. For assistance with that, we strongly encourage you to read a different book. Any other book, literally. Sometimes saying very little actually means knowing when to say absolutely nothing. Confused yet?

Being personal and approachable would seem by default to involve at the very least verbal communication. However, because they have such attuned listening skills, they are patient and spend time gathering information before communicating back with a thoughtful response.

Connectors realize that oftentimes, especially if someone is having a problem, they just need to listen to that person. After listening, concise, reflective questions are a common response from Connectors as they oftentimes lead the other person to determine the answer on their own. And, at times, the less a Connector says, the more of an impact they have. So, maybe your spouse was actually listening when they didn't respond to you? Or, at least give him until the commercial break before you make up your mind.

Finally, people are drawn to Connectors because they typically feel better after interacting with them. Connectors seem to almost have a gravitational pull around them. As we stated previously, some staff will go out of their way, consciously or not, to be close to the Connector just because it makes them feel good. Connectors believe that, 99 percent of the time, the interactions they have with others should make them (students, staff, whomever) feel as good or better as compared to before the interaction.

In this way, Connectors can have a powerful effect on people close to them, which in turn can result in a powerful effect on many others. **Connectors are personable and approachable, and they use this as leverage to have a positive impact in your school**. So, bust out the magnets (but don't get them too close to the computers-bad things will happen, trust me). Who can you pull in?

## TRUST IS EARNED AND VALUED ("VALYOUD")

You've heard of "There is no 'I' in 'TEAM,'" but how about "There must be '**US**' in 'TRUST.'" Do you like it? You can have it, for free (mostly because it's not ours!). You can also have "Val**you**d," for the same reason.

We spoke earlier in this chapter about how respect is earned. We'd argue that trust is similar in that most of us are somewhat automatically trustworthy of others. Trust is the key ingredient for Connectors and their focus on relationships. They know that they must invest much time and energy into gaining trust from others through their words and actions. They are also fully aware of just how quickly trust can be broken. Connectors treat the concept of trust with high regard and value its power.

The pace of building trust often starts slowly. **The receiver, not the Connector, typically controls the pace that trust is earned and maintained**. Students, especially at the secondary level, can be guarded and only willing to give small pieces of information out before feeling comfortable to share more. Some of your colleagues are the same.

Connectors understand this and look at building trust as a marathon, not a sprint. Said another way, they view trust as a puzzle. Every situation where the Connector is given another piece of the puzzle gets them one step closer to getting the complete picture. Like a puzzle, trust is built one piece at a time. (Geez, first a magnet, now a puzzle. What's next, a "Connect the Dots" reference?)

> There was one student I taught for only one year who was quite challenging. I really tried to get to know him for who he was and focus on all the great things that made him special. I tried hard to build a trusting relationship with him. We began to talk more, he began to open up to me more, and we began to smile more. (Erica, elementary teacher)

A Connector assesses themselves differently than other COREs. Rather than asking themselves who they collaborated with (which, for the record, is a good question to ask), they might ask themselves, *"What relationships did I improve today?"* And instead of asking what they may have taught someone that day (another good question), they might ask, *"Who did I connect with on a new level today?"* I'd like to share a personal story that is an example of how years ago I should have been asking myself these questions, but wasn't.

I had a shift in my professional practice early on as a school counselor, but it wasn't due to one of my official duties in that role. Rather, the lesson on the power of trust came as a swimming coach. To all the coaches and activity/club leaders out there, you know that the best connections you make with kids are oftentimes outside of the classroom. For me, it happened in a few years of coaching high school swimming.

I had an athlete named "Josh," who also happened to be assigned to my caseload as a school counselor. Well, during his sophomore year, Josh and I had regular interactions due to some minor difficulties in a few of his classes, but that was about it. From the little I knew of Josh, he was a "typical" high school kid, with some struggles and frustrations outside of school, but nothing out of the ordinary. I noticed that, whenever I tried to steer our discussions about academic problems to his life outside of school, however, he would quickly redirect them back to school.

All of that changed once I became his swimming coach. Many, many practices, meets, and long bus rides provided numerous opportunities to get to know Josh and "his story." He let me know about how his mom had to work three jobs to keep the heat on in their apartment. He let me know that he was late to first hour a lot because he had to walk his little sister to school every day because his mom was at work. He let me know that he never really had his dad around, or any type of positive male figure in his life. And, perhaps most importantly, he let me know his hopes and dreams. He let me in. We were connecting.

From then on, we moved our conversations away from what had happened to him in the past to where he wanted to go and what he wanted to be. Years later, Josh couldn't believe when he got accepted into technical college. Not only was he going to be the first person in his family to graduate with a high school diploma, but he was also on his way to college. On graduation day, he thanked me for helping to get him there. I reminded him that he had done the work. And, it was all made possible by . . . trust (and hard work, including swimming endless laps while looking at the bottom of the swimming pool for longer than anyone should have to).

Educator: Play a round of the classic game "Connect 4" (available free online as well) with a student who needs you to build a stronger relationship with them. For every time you drop a checker (or perhaps just each time someone wins a game), share something about yourself and vice versa.

Leader: The next time a staff person comes to you with a problem that they want you to solve, don't give them the answer. Just listen. Be patient and see if they can come to the solution on their own. Though they won't realize it at the time, you'll be building a connection along the way.

As we wrap up this portion of the chapter, we'd like to leave you with this quote that we believe captures the essence of the Connector CORE. After reading it, take a moment to reflect:

*In our final moments we all realize that relationships are what life is all about. Wisdom is learning that truth sooner rather than later.* (Warren, 2002)

Ask yourself this question: *Where am I in realizing this?* And *Who specifically can I reach out to in this moment today to make sure I'm not regretting the relationship in my final moments?* If doing this hit you like a punch in the stomach, that was intentional.

## SUMMARY

We define a person who is strong in the Connector CORE as someone who "understands and is committed to the strength of relationships with people."

We believe that those staff in the school where you work each day have the following four characteristics in common:

- Relationships are the Foundation
- Genuine Care for Others
- Personable and Approachable
- Trust is Earned and Valued ("Val**you**d")

Here's the "Connect the dots" point which was referenced earlier that you know you were waiting for. "Connect the dots" is defined on Wikipedia as "a form of puzzle containing a sequence of numbered dots. When a line is drawn connecting the dots the outline of an object is revealed" (wikipedia.org). The authors of the book say this, "Exactly." Not all that profound, but we're just two normal (sort of) dudes from Wisconsin.

Let's explain further. The Connector is a master of connect the dots puzzles. They are able to draw the invisible lines to make connections with others, and to help others make connections with still others. The "object that is revealed"; in this case, strong relationships with others, doesn't come by happenstance but rather by hard work and by keeping the end in mind.

For Connectors, the end in mind means many things. First and foremost, it's always about relationships. Always. They have a clear picture of where their relationships need to be to get results, what steps to take to get there, and how to put those steps into action. Speaking of results, educators strong in the Connector CORE are all about results.

The authors of this book, while admittedly still a work in progress for other COREs, would humbly suggest that their strength in the Connector CORE, in their ability to build relationships, has been critical to increasing student achievement in their varied roles over a combined forty-plus years in education.

Connectors care deeply for others. They don't just take the time in the moment to build relationships, they're strategic and intentional about making the time. And, they'll even schedule it. Whether it's asking about a colleagues weekend (and actually listening and responding to what they say), discussing with a student how their game went the previous evening, or going out of their way to do something kind for another, it's their genuine care for others that sets them apart.

Connectors have an innate ability to relate to other people in a way that makes them feel accepted and valued. They put people first. *Yeah, agreed.* They put the "us" in trust. *Yeah, catchy.* (Stay with this.) Essentially, they invest in people, not things. *Yeah, makes sense.* They invest in building a strong foundation with others. *Yeah, got it.* They are like the third little pig.

*Wait, what?* The third little pig built his house of bricks, right? He, quite literally connected all three pigs together into one safe home. That third little (Connector) pig literally saved their lives—or at least prevented them from being served for dinner on that day. So, by extension, Connectors quite literally can be lifesavers because they believe in strong foundations. *"Corny?"* Yes. Or, would that be *"Piggy?"*

## Perspective-Taking Scenario

The police liaison officer in your building, or the one who is assigned to your building and who you see on occasion, doesn't seem to be doing what you believe he's supposed to be doing (though you admittedly aren't sure what that is). When you do see him (in between classes when you take three minutes to actually go to the bathroom), he's high-fiving kids in the hallway. Literally. Oh, and what's that, he's smiling from ear to ear again as he chats them up. Doesn't he have something else he should be doing? When you were a kid, police officers were somewhat feared, or at the very least conducted themselves in a manner that demanded respect.

Not this goofball. What in the world does he do all day? Shouldn't he be disciplining students, or writing tickets, or handing out baseball cards, or, . . .something. If you had more time, you'd ask your colleagues about him. But you don't, the bell is going to ring again and you've got to get back to work. Speaking of work, when is he going to start? So, now what should you do? Choose from the responses below:

A. Continue to wonder what he does, and resent him along the way
B. Ask a colleague about him, as perhaps they'll know
C. Tell the principal on him (refer to "snitches get stitches" comment earlier)
D. Talk with the police officer; perhaps he'll give you some perspective

Hint: The answer is NOT "A" or "C." "D" is likely the best answer, but "B" will also keep you out of the emergency room.

## CORE Questions to Consider

1. Do you believe that educators who value relationships have students who achieve higher academically because of it? Why or why not?
2. Who is the most personable and approachable staff member you know? How do they make you feel? How do they make students feel?

3. Is there more or less of a need to build relationships with students at the secondary level as compared to the elementary level?

**We Dare You Challenge**

The Connector CORE is all about relationships. Consider the relationship that you have with one colleague, a relationship that you would like to improve. Think about what you have in common that you could build from. What actions could you take to leverage those commonalities and thus improve the relationship? Make a plan, write it down if you have to. Now go do it. (Seriously, now. What are you waiting for? Or, would you just like to keep doing the same thing that you have been doing and getting the same results?) Go on. We dare you.

**Now What?/Action Steps**

If this is your CORE, you should use it for the following actions:

- Build time into your day to check in on colleagues
- Genuinely listen
- Know everyone's name
- Build fun into your time with people through words and actions

Why Every Team Needs Someone with the Connector CORE

- To use the mutual trust built to foster a feeling of "we're all in this together"
- To create a safe and supportive learning environment
- To make the work seem, well . . . less like work
- To recognize, value, and connect to the human element of education

How Identifying People with the Connector CORE Helps My School Leader

- Knows that strong relationships with students will positively impact achievement
- Helps leaders see the significance of relationships in the real world/workforce
- Models how to build relationships with others
- Offers balance to the leaders who may be naturally and solely academically focused
- Supports staff retention

How Understanding the Connector CORE Helps Me Understand My Colleagues

- Achieves more with students through trusting relationships
- Showing genuine care actually relieves pressure kids feel to perform
- It's relationships that make the biggest difference when things get tough
- The "cool" teacher is often not really cool, they just care (which is VERY cool)

*Chapter 7*

# Energizer

**Energizer:** spreads their positive attitude, joy, and fun in all they do

*What we learn with pleasure we never forget.*

—Alfred Mercier

"You can do it brother! Just keep pumping, like this. I think this is what grownups mean when they talk about joy. We'll be chasing this feeling our whole lives. Hey, by the way, why didn't mom and dad put clothes on us today . . . again?"

## PERSONAL STORY

The Energizer is all about a positive attitude and having fun. Most often (hopefully), we get to experience the fun ourselves. Sometimes, however, others have the fun at our expense. This is a story of the latter.

We've shared glimpses into the deep, dark, manipulative minds of our older brothers before. Don't get us wrong, we love them. But, for the sake of our stories, we need to villainize them a little bit. It makes it more fun . . . and that's the focus of the Energizer chapter . . . FUN.

Like most stories, this one works best if we set the scene. We were ten years old and having a sleepover. Many of our stories seem to include our childhood friends. Looking back, I think it's because our older brothers, typically Jeff, would be better able to hone his skills on multiple targets, I mean, friends. From a distance, and with time, you really have to appreciate his body of work. And, as you'll see later in this story, "targets" (and "bodies") are the perfect word to use.

Let's get back to the sleepover. Since parents of four boys can only really survive if they can get their children out of the house for as much time as possible, we spent a lot of time outdoors in our yard. On this particular day, we were in our fenced-in backyard playing some random game neither of us can remember. In comparison to most yards, ours was a fairly large lot, but still very contained and leaving few routes for escape.

Anyways, we were in the backyard playing, and I suddenly felt a sharp stinging on the left side of my face, near my neck. "*Ouch. What was that?*" Maybe a bee or something? Not sure, I thought, just keep playing. About thirty seconds later, "*OUCH*," another one. After another few minutes, I was hit again. Ok, what's going on here? I looked around to see our friends rubbing their arms, legs, heads, and one kid got hit just below the eye. "*What IS going on here?*" we all thought.

While rubbing the pain out of my right forearm, I noticed a distinct smell. It smelled like my mom when she and dad would go out for a rare night out (or to a funeral). Yeah, that's it. That's the smell. It was . . . WOMEN'S PERFUME!

But how? And why? Imagine my confusion as I was both in pain and smelling of women's perfume that was on my body, wondering what the source of both were. Just then, out of the corner of my eye, I noticed movement in our brother's second-floor bedroom window. It was brief, but it appeared to be something being quickly brought back into the house, through a small hole in the screen. But, what was it?

Still confused (and a little dazed from being pelted by some foreign objects that smelled of liberally applied perfume), I looked down and saw the backyard littered with mysterious small, white objects no bigger than my pinky. *What in the world?* I picked one up. Q-tips? But why? I smelled one. It smelled like an old lady (sorry mom). They were q-tips dipped in our mother's perfume! It was all coming together.

Our older brother had been using his blowdart gun to shoot us with q-tips dipped in perfume from his bedroom window! For those of you who don't know what a blowdart gun is, Google it. And, consider yourself lucky. It's not as dangerous as Ralphie's Red Ryder BB gun in the classic movie, "A Christmas Story," but still makes for a great story.

As we realized what had happened, we rushed toward the house (all reeking of perfume and having several small red welts on our bodies) to seek revenge (and cover). But, all of the doors were locked! Coincidence? We don't think so. By the time we got our parents to answer the door, our brother had disposed of all of the evidence, hopped on his bike and made a clean getaway. And, he wouldn't be back to the house until late that night when we had all fallen fast asleep. We knew that any attempts to tell our parents would only eventually lead to additional "consequences" from our brother. So, once again, we had no other recourse than to move on with our day (and shower).

The Energizer is all about fun and our brother had surely achieved it . . . even if it was at our expense. You stink Jeff. Or, wait a minute, that might still be us.

## ENERGIZER DEFINED

We define a person who is strong in the Energizer CORE as someone who "spreads their positive attitude, joy and fun in all they do." As we said earlier in the personal story that "reeked" (see what we did there) of perfume, the Energizer "reeks" of fun. It's also about spreading positive energy—after all, "energy" is pretty much quite literally in the core of the word.

**The Energizer is all about having a positive mindset.** It's that simple. We could stop there, but that would make for a pretty boring read. But, we could. Energizers are all about attitude. And, they choose to have a positive one, even if at times it can be kind of annoying or at the very least, confusing. Who do these people think they are? Why do they get to come to work every day and be happy, acting like there is nothing in the world to worry about? They must not have any problems in their lives. They must be the teachers who have classes full of all of the "good" kids. They must be the principal with all of the "good" teachers. Must be nice. They can't possibly have the personal or professional stresses that you endure. Or, is it something else? Yes, **Energizers CHOOSE to view their lives through a positive lens.** That's why they are so joyful.

Energizers know that when they constantly look for the good in things, people, and situations, and they are their happiest and most fulfilled. Perhaps the best part is that this comes so naturally for them; it's just how they get out of bed each morning (plus perhaps a cup of coffee, or four).

Being an Energizer starts with how you view yourself. It's in your attitude. It's in your mindset. What better book to reference than arguably the most influential book ever written about this topic, *Mindset*, by Carol Dweck. She states, "The view you adopt of yourself profoundly affects the way you lead your life. It can determine whether you become the person you want to be and whether you accomplish the things you value" (Dweck, 2006). While Dweck offers this perspective relative to growth or fixed mindsets, we offer it through the lens of a positive or less-than-positive *attitude* and how you can spread that attitude to others in the school that you work in.

Here's a question to reflect on: How many people with negative attitudes do you know who are fulfilled in their lives? There is a direct correlation there, right? **People who view themselves and the situations around them in a positive light have a better chance of both achieving their goals and feeling satisfied in life.** I'm not sure anyone would argue that. But, if it's that simple, why doesn't everyone see that and change their attitude? Or, perhaps they don't know how? Or, they don't think they have the power to change it? Great questions . . . and perhaps the topic of another book.

For the Energizer, it's about having joy, being positive, and spreading joy to others along the way. We believe that the CORE of the Energizer can best be further defined by breaking our definition down into four main subcategories as outlined below:

- Joy in Everything for Today
- Positive Outlook for Tomorrow
- Motivates and Models with Enthusiasm
- Effectively Manages Stress

## JOY IN EVERYTHING FOR TODAY

If you look hard enough, you can find some amount of joy in almost anything. Yes, even . . . work! Crazy talk? We think not. We know it's called "going to work" and not "going to joy" for a reason, but still. There's joy everywhere. Even, and perhaps especially, at work. You might as well make it joyful, as you're there for most of your waking hours, five days a week, right? Since this book is written by educators, for educators, we too share the many struggles that we all have as teachers and leaders in a school or district. We're right there with you. However, **there is joy, everywhere, every day**. It's all around you. Sometimes, though, it's hard to see. We'd submit, however, that it's there if you look for it . . . and if you choose to see it.

**Energizers find and insert joy into everything they do**. And, thank goodness for them. We've all found ourselves drawn to this person far more times than we have found ourselves drawn away. In this way, they're similar to Connectors. Simply put, Energizers BRING IT every day. Somehow they seem to generate the energy to possess and bring joy into most every situation and interaction.

This is the person who genuinely smiles at you in the hallway first thing in the morning, shares a positive spin on a tough situation during a staff meeting, or seems to enjoy (or at the very least not be bothered by) staying later to meet with parents on parent-teacher conference nights. How are they so joyful all of the time? Don't they see the barriers and struggles right in front of us? Shouldn't they take things more seriously? Or, are they more concerned with having fun than getting real results in terms of growth for kids? What's wrong with them? (rhetorical question, please).

Here are the answers. Energizers do take things seriously. For them, the obstacles ahead are crystal clear. And, they are very concerned with results. However, they simply take a different approach to things. They are truly and genuinely happy, both naturally and by choice, each day.

Dave Burgess, fellow educator and poster child for the Energizer CORE, wrote about teaching with joy, in *Teach Like a Pirate*. He stated, "I'll always choose a teacher with enthusiasm and weak technique over one with brilliant strategies but who is just punching the clock. Why? An enthusiastic teacher can learn technique, but it is almost impossible to light a fire inside the charred heart of a burned-out teacher."

To his point, we all want to be around teachers who teach with joy. For those of us who currently have or have had our own school-aged children, we want them to be taught by teachers who exhibit joy in the classroom everyday. Why? Because we want to see (and feel) the joy that our own kids have about school every night when we ask them about it. **Enthusiasm trumps technique**. Period.

Educator: Ask your students, formally or informally, about what they like to do for fun. When reviewing the answers, look for common themes, then offer opportunities to experience that fun and energy in your lessons. Be creative.

Leader: When hiring, consider the candidate's genuine level of energy and enthusiasm. If it's absent during the interview, it's likely to be absent each of the 180ish days of classroom instruction.

If we see the immense value in this for our biological children, then why aren't we doing everything we possibly can to provide for the ones in our own classroom? The Energizer CORE spreads positive energy, joy, and fun just like the "pirate" teacher. In a way, this transcends even the content that is being taught or the work to be done. **Start with joy** in the work (whether it be in the classroom, on the playground, or in the administrative office), **and the engagement in the content will naturally follow**.

> I am blessed, I am lucky, and I feel like I can and will be a teacher who changes kids lives forever. (Erica, elementary teacher)

Let's talk about finding joy connected to getting positive results for students. **Real Energizers leverage fun, to lessen pressure, to get results.** There's a lot there. Do yourself a favor and reread and reflect on that sentence.

Now, let's face it, there are colleagues we work with who are fun and who bring a lighthearted attitude to work every day. We might like being around them and they do have somewhat of a positive effect on the overall work environment. But we'd argue that unless it yields academic results, then they are not complete Energizers. If you feel like you are a complete Energizer, how do the academic results of your students compare to those of the other teachers in your building or district? If they are the same or higher, good. If not, then you are not successfully leveraging fun, to lessen the pressure, to get results. It's no good if you're the "cool" third grade teacher, or the "funny" science teacher, or the teacher every kid asks to be assigned to your class, if it doesn't lead to increased student achievement. Sorry. Or, are we?

If you can reflect and determine that while you do bring joy into your classroom but fail to get higher academic results than your colleagues, the good news is that you have the foundational pieces for success. Remember, Dave Burgess would rather work with you than some of your colleagues! And, to be honest, it's the positive environment that you've created that allows for the next step toward increasing student engagement and achievement. You know what you need to do next to bring it home!

Here is a quick story about a simple way to inject fun into the school day. And, for the record, I stole this idea from another school so please feel free to steal it from me.

What's one of the more annoying sounds in a school? No, not the principal's voice over the PA system (well, maybe). No, not nails on a chalkboard (not as funny for younger educators since they may have never heard this). The answer is: the bells or tones that schools use to announce passing times, recess, and so on.

Here's a solution to inject joy: connect a laptop or phone to your PA system and use music to remind students of what's happening next in the school day or to play a song that has some meaning to your students. And, have fun with it. For elementary schools, choose different songs for different activities or different parts of the day. Find a fun song to let them know it's time to line up to come in from the playground, one that tells them it's time for lunch, one to leave classes for your school-wide community meetings, and so on.

For secondary schools with set passing times by period for all, have a song playing for that exact amount of time. When the song ends, let's say after the four minutes allowed for passing, everyone needs to be in their classes. You might be thinking, "This won't work in my classroom or school." Think again. Some deviation of it will. Make it work. Give it a try. Find joy. Create a memory for your students. Surprise your students and do it once. See what happens. What do you have to lose?

One final note about how this can work in a school: We have a lot of fun at my high school by switching up the songs every once and awhile. You can even select songs by the time of year or holiday that is approaching. Who doesn't LOVE hearing a Michael Jackson "Thriller" instrumental blaring through the hallway speakers around Halloween time? Or a fun song announcing that it's Friday? Enjoy it. It's amazing how the combination of a number of small, yet fun, things (even as simple as songs over the announcements) can add up to make a big impact on the level of joy at your school.

## POSITIVE OUTLOOK FOR TOMORROW

We believe that there are differences between being joyful and having a positive outlook. It's why we made them each into their own, separate portions of this book. There are overlaps and similarities, but they are different. In the section on joy, we stated that joy happens in the present tense. We see and notice joy right in front of us all the time, and it can be energizing in the moment. Positive outlook, on the other hand, offers something different. **Positive outlook is about the future, the long term.** It occurs as part of a bigger picture that is comprised of many smaller components (like joy in the moment over and over and over so frequently that it becomes almost expected to continue to occur in the future). Enter "Positive Outlook for Tomorrow."

George Couros has said many times, "We need to make the positives so loud, that the negatives are almost impossible to hear." Energizers have a positive outlook that doesn't allow the negative to take over. **Energizers make intentional efforts to block the potential impact of negative influences.** Skilled Energizers also have the ability to overpower negative impacts and change the trajectory to a positive, or at least a neutral, one. When you consider this, you can probably think of times in your life when a positive person may not have "changed the negative to a positive," but they at least lessened its impact or neutralized it completely.

A good example of an Energizer in schools is the staff person who hears a problem and doesn't allow themselves to get sucked into the great abyss of complaining about it without offering a solution. They hear and recognize the issue, but shift gears to a focus on solving the problem. At a staff meeting where the mention of a prevalent school issue is brought up, they are the ones who insert themselves with an idea for a potential solution. Like Couros says, **Energizers make the negatives almost impossible to hear**.

Breaux and Whitaker concur when they write, "The very best teachers agree that attitude is everything! One of the main things that separate the not-so-good from the good from the great teachers is simply attitude" (2006). This is what we wrote about in one of the first sentences of this chapter when we defined the Energizer CORE. We stated that the Energizer is all about mindset. How simple. And, something we can all control.

As we wrap up the Positive Outlook section of this chapter, we wanted to share a perspective that we have about this topic as much or more about life as it is about school. Here goes.

We know that the Energizer brings a positive outlook for the future to everything due to their positive attitude. On a related note, the authors believe that far too many people look to some future magical date when (insert option from below here), life will be much better, instead of living for today. (Here's where we get onto the soap box of life, not necessarily education.)

Options for when life will be easier include:

- The quarter, semester, or school year is over
- Winter is over and the snow finally melts (we're jealous of all of you who can't relate to this, although "snow days" where school is canceled are quite nice)
- All of your own kids are (finally) out of diapers
- The (insert sport here) season is over and we don't have to drive our children around seemingly every night and weekends to practices and games
- I get this certain promotion or job
- The kids are out of the house
- I retire . . . (that one might be as great as expected, holding out hope. . . . )

The reality is, **today is the day for joy** (and to have a positive outlook for tomorrow). Today is a gift. Not only are there no guarantees about tomorrow, there are also no guarantees that tomorrow (or next year or five years from now) will be as magical as you expect them to be based on the options above. So, like the Energizer does, live for today and know that tomorrow will be just as good or better. *What's good about TODAY?* It's there, no matter what day it is.

This is a positive mindset and the best lens to view life. Which mindset do you want to live in today to help support a positive outlook for tomorrow?

## MOTIVATES AND MODELS WITH ENTHUSIASM

Perhaps the best quote to use to start this section is one from two very well-known scholars in academia, Hans and Franz from the show *Saturday Night Live* (back in the 1980s, when it was really good). They were bodybuilders who very eloquently and jointly said, *"We're here to pump* (insert clap), *YOU UP!"* **Energizers** (*like Hans and Franz*) **motivate others and model positivity by spreading joy in everything they do.** And, they do it without even trying.

They do it by simply being themselves. Just how most educators agree with the concept that kids know if you care, we'd argue that kids (and adults) know if you are genuinely enthusiastic ("pumped up") or not. They know if you possess joy, the kind of joy that somehow makes others feel better after they've talked to you. This comes out in nearly every interaction they have with people. Kids recognize it and know it nearly instantaneously with school staff. Do they recognize it in you? The Energizer, regardless of their role, has the ability to affect the entire school environment simply by motivating and modeling with enthusiasm. Crazy powerful, hey? They don't need to necessarily be an extrovert or hold a leadership position in a school building. They could easily be an introvert with other adults, but have a strength in building strong relationships with students through modeling their positive attitude. You'll find an example of this in the next paragraph.

Have you ever been a part of a larger school staff where you didn't ever really get to know every staff member in your building that well? Most educators can relate in some way. There might be a few quiet staff who are friendly, but pretty much keep to themselves or to a small group of colleagues. We often think of those colleagues as unassertive and certainly unlikely to be motivational.

Then, we happen to walk past their room one day and hear joy, laughter, and fun bursting from their room. The voice in front of the class, although you can't see the person, is loud, confident, funny, and engaging. You realize that the enthusiastic voice is coming from that quiet and unassuming teacher who you thought likely was similar in the classroom as they are in other settings. But how? The point is that Energizers can show this strength in certain areas of their lives, but less in others. An introvert CAN be an Energizer. Does that describe you or someone you know?

Educator: Think about what percentage of your work week that you bring a positive attitude (lots of energy) to. Now, commit to increasing that by 10% this week simply by telling yourself that you have control of it. Like a colleague of mine says, "Make it a great day." You are absolutely in control.

Leader: We've already discussed the strength of modeling the behavior we want to see in others. Be intentionally super positive this week and see how others respond to you. (If they seem to be giving you funny looks, then consider the necessity to extend this beyond the week!)

Since the CORE of Energizer by our definition has both the words "joy" and "fun" in it, I'd like to share a story about one particular lesson that brings me great joy as a teacher and I'm hoping is fun for the students as well.

Each year in first grade as part of our math curriculum I teach 3D objects. This can be challenging for some students, who want to call a sphere a circle, a cube a box, and so on. After years of trying to teach kids these math terms using ineffective instructional strategies like repeatedly saying the same object names over and over (and over and over), saying it louder and withholding snack until they memorized the words (made that last one up), I decided to try a new technique.

One day, when holding a sphere, cylinder, and a cube in my hands and holding one at a time up for the kids to call out what the 3D object name was, it dawned on me that I could capitalize on a skill that I learned during my five and a half short years of undergraduate school, juggling. Money well spent.

As I was holding the three objects, it dawned on me that I could attempt to juggle these shapes, doing so intentionally slowly by throwing the objects higher up into the air than normal, and having the kids say the object that was flying through the air as it reached its peak. I told the kids the order in which the three objects would be flying so they could get the words in their heads, and then slowly threw them up in the air using this slower rhythm.

The kids could be heard saying; *"Sphere, cylinder, cube . . . Sphere, cylinder, cube . . . ."* It was awesome, or at least better than most lessons I've done. While I'm not sure if all of those students could still today recite those 3D object names upon request, I am quite sure that they remembered that day when their parents asked them what they did at school (and maybe if they had the delicious chicken nuggets for hot lunch).

There was joy and fun in this lesson, and the enthusiasm the kids had for the lesson was through the roof. That's what someone with the Energizer CORE does.

> Education is the golden key to open doors to opportunities and places never dreamed of. I want to help students find the right key for them. (Chris, elementary teacher)

For Energizers, it's all about attitude. That is, choosing a positive attitude each day and modeling that choice for others. "We are the teachers. We are the leaders. We are the role models. Every day, our attitudes help to shape the types of teachers, leaders, and role models we become" (Breaux & Whitaker, 2006).

Like it or not, our individual actions affect more than simply who we are or who we become. They affect the attitudes and actions of everyone around us, including and especially our students. **There is no stronger way to influence others than by modeling the behavior you hope to see**. Think about it. We grow up and learn by mimicking those around us. At younger ages, we may not have the capacity to know whether the actions that we are essentially copying are the appropriate ones, but we incorporate them into who we are because that is what is being modeled for us. What are you modeling for those around you each day?

Breaux and Whitaker go on to say, "One person really can make a difference—so be that one person. Shape up your attitude, and your students will remember you with gratitude" (pg. 78). And, students will remember. In fact, if you think about it, you may even remember a teacher Energizer you had in school (way back when you had to walk every day to and from school in the snow . . . uphill . . . both ways). Likely, you remember them for their energy, the positiveness that surrounds them. Respectfully, do you remember them more for that, even over the content that they taught you? It all starts with shaping your attitude. This quote highlights that students most certainly recognize the attitude that we bring to school each day.

We've often wondered how it is that some teachers, even those in the same grade level or department, can have such vastly different levels of enthusiasm including their attitudes. After all, their workloads are essentially the same. They each have approximately the same number of students, the same amount of lessons to prepare, the same parent issues, the same amount of meetings, and so on. (As a sidenote, know that we understand that there can be a difference in those two teachers' lives outside of school, with times in their life that are truly very difficult for other reasons. But, don't let that be a cop-out for you. Those difficult times don't last forever. In fact, the most positive person goes through those terrible personal times too, you just may not know about it.)

So, how is it that these two teachers' attitudes can be at two totally different ends of the spectrum? Our simple answer is that it's all about CHOICE. That's right; they simply *choose* each morning to bring a positive attitude to work every day and motivate others by modeling that energetic attitude. While this may not be earth-shattering information to you, it's worth taking a moment to reflect on the attitude that you choose each day.

The next time you're casually asked, *"How are you today?"*, what will you answer? *OK, good, doing fine* are the likely responses. Try this . . . *"As good as I CHOOSE to be!"* Wait for the double take. Not only have you just made your colleague think and reflect, you've also spread the Energizer joy! Remember to "Motivate and Model with Enthusiasm" every day! *Disclaimer: The authors of this book are not responsible for the numerous Hans and Franz videos you've watched or plan to watch since reading this subsection of the book.* It's only funny because it's true.

## EFFECTIVELY MANAGES STRESS

The Energizer often appears to be stress free. They aren't, of course, but there is a calming presence about them that makes us feel that they must certainly not be dealing with the same pressures that we are. Right? We touched on this briefly earlier. Why don't they have the "tough" kids assigned to their classroom? Why don't they seem stressed about the district assessments coming up? Were they not pelted with perfume-soaked q-tips as children and have lasting stressors associated with constant reminders when they walk into the perfume section at a store in the mall? One thing is for sure; they must have it easier than others. Or, do they just manage the stressors of work (and life) differently?

It's difficult for some of us to admit, but some colleagues simply manage stress better than others. The positive outlook on life that Energizers possess promotes healthy life balance. They've created routines and habits in their lives that may not seem directly related to their jobs, but when successfully executed over time have a positive impact.

Think of the Energizers in your life. Now, think of the things they do outside of school. What are their hobbies? What do they do in their spare time? Energizers have intentionally inserted numerous other important aspects of their lives beyond work that support effective management of the same stress that others struggle with.

**Energizers don't typically sweat the small stuff**. They care about outcomes just as much you do, but they choose to get there while traveling down a less-stressful path. Read this quote with a lens of an Energizer, someone who handles stress well, even if that's not typically you:

> "You are generous with praise, quick to smile, and always on the lookout for the positive in the situation. Some call you lighthearted. Others just wish that their glass were as full as yours seems to be. You celebrate every achievement. You find ways to make everything more exciting and more vital. . . . Somehow you can't quite escape your conviction that it's good to be alive, that work can be fun, and that no matter what the setbacks, one must never lose one's sense of humor" (Buckingham & Clifton 2001).

How did that feel? Great, right? That's how an Energizer feels nearly every day. As educators, there are many struggles and stressors, every day and every hour. As a teacher, how can you meet the needs of all of my readers who are at such different levels? As an aide, how can you effectively manage all of the behaviors at lunch? As a principal, how can you support a teacher but also show parents that you hear their concern? As a district office person, how can you support instruction in schools and also work with outside groups who want to "add" something meaningful to the school system? The stress is real.

As the quote states, there are many ways the Energizer manages this stress. The good news is, what they do takes no preparation. Reread the quote, and you'll see what we mean. *Generous with praise . . . smile . . . on the lookout for the positive. . . .* Energizers manage their stress, they're strategic about doing so, and they live a healthier life because of it. And, it takes no time. Which is good, because as an educator, you don't have any!

| Educator: Learn mindful practices like deep breathing or guided imagery to manage your stress. Focus on one of these tomorrow, then another the next day. When you get good at it, start them with your classes or students you serve. |
|---|
| Leader: Start every staff meeting with a "Mindful Minute." Make it a routine. The same staff who initially think that it's hokey might just become the ones who complain if you ever mistakenly start a meeting without it. |

This reminds me of my first year as a principal, and is initially more of a non-example about effectively managing stress. I was awful in my job at first and I knew it. It's true. I stressed about every little thing. I worked way longer hours than I should have and was very inefficient. I worked harder at trying to please people rather than doing the right thing. Following a few months of being out of my exercise routine (after all, who has time to exercise when you're too busy running a school seventy hours per week), I decided to return to a regular morning basketball game with a group of teachers.

I recall the first time I went back. That hour was a powerful experience for me. As I was walking off the court, it hit me: I had just gone one full hour without stressing about work. I felt reenergized and focused. It was as if I had the most restful sleep of my life and had awoken ready to take on any challenge. I was a new person.

I had been in such a deep rut that I wasn't capable of even recognizing the unhealthy position that I had put myself in or how that had negatively affected my outlook on life, as well as my job performance. It was life-changing for me. For our reader, here's a question: *What do you do that is a healthy distraction from your job?* If you've strayed away from it, *What commitment are you willing to make to return to it? How might it change you?* Hint: You're reading a chapter called the Energizer!

For our students, clear minds lead to innovative, fun, and creative ideas. As school staff, we need to create learning environments where we minimize stress for kids. That is not to say that there should be no stress at all. We are not suggesting that school staff should remove all pressure from kids to succeed. After all, some of you are thinking in your heads right now that the real world is full of stress and pressure and we need to prepare our students for that. We agree, to some extent. In schools, however, we refer to adding pressure on kids as having "high expectations" for them. Call it what you want, the truth is that these high expectations put pressure on kids (for good and for bad).

*Energizer*

Our position is that **Energizers have a tactful way of relieving some (not all) pressure in the classroom by injecting fun, which then leads to an environment that promotes both personal and academic growth.** They know how to differentiate between stress that can be character-building from stress that can be unnecessary or even harmful. Bottom line, kids perform best with some stress, but also some relief of pressure through enjoying the learning experience. That's right, we said, "enjoying the learning experience." Learning should be enjoyable. There are other ways to prepare students for the "real world." In the classroom, or whatever your role is as an educator, and in your life, you'll actually experience more successes by choosing some fun from time to time over more work which causes undue stress. Working 24/7 isn't helping and it's not healthy. The Energizer knows that. Do you?

## SUMMARY

You know that person you work with who is always happy, always filled with energy? They seem to have a great attitude about everything. They are filled with joy, and spread it like wildfire. People want to be around them in hopes that some of it will magically rub off on them. Most of you love them, but a little part of you isn't quite sure it's legit. Well, it is. They're Energizers. I wonder: Would referencing the "Energizer Bunny" be too much here? Or, is it already too late to wonder that?

As stated in this chapter, the Energizer is all about mindset. This staff member has the same or similar stressors as others, yet they choose to view their work and personal lives through a positive lens.

We broke down this chapter about those strong in the Energizer CORE into four main sections:

- Joy in Everything for Today
- Positive Outlook for Tomorrow
- Motivates and Models with Enthusiasm
- Effectively Manages Stress

If you read this chapter and thought that this isn't a CORE that you're strong in, that's ok. We would recommend that you spend more time with the Energizers in your school. They will turn negative situations into positive ones, they'll find joy in everything they do, they'll leverage fun to get positive results for kids, and in their own way they'll be modeling that behavior to influence others. You.

## Perspective-Taking Scenario

You walk into the teacher's lounge during your lunch break (which means you have about thirteen minutes to scarf down last night's leftovers), and there is a teacher complaining about the parent of a student in their classroom. He's saying that the parent is claiming that their child is not being challenged enough. You also have this student for class and the same parent who also reached out to you via email about not challenging their daughter. The student does pick up quickly on the math content of your class so you've found some ways to easily offer her more advanced work without compromising more than a few minutes of your time. Choose your own adventure as to how you respond to this teacher:

- Choice #1: You microwave the overcooked pasta from last night's dinner and high-tail it out of the lounge like the place is on fire.
- Choice #2: You sit down as your normally would, and listen and half nod in some sort of weird agreement (or is it just out of habit and the fact that you now have just eleven minutes to eat your lunch?) as he continues his story.
- Choice #3: You share that you have that same student, and also had the parent inquire via email about the very same topic. You then share one or two things you've done for the child, including offering that it really wasn't any more work for you. Perhaps you say that the parent even emailed back a few words of thanks (or at least stopped emailing at all!).

## Which one do you choose?

Hint, chose # 3. Now, reflect. How did your sharing your positive energy impact your colleague, the student, their parents, others in the lounge, and you? That's a lot of impact! And, with the now "extra" four minutes that you have remaining for lunch, sit back and relax while watching another episode of SNL and "Pumping Up, with Hans and Franz" all while reflecting on the positive energy that you spread!

## CORE Questions to Consider

1. Who is the most positive person on your staff? Did you name yourself? If so, why? If not, why not? Assuming you answered someone else, how specifically does that person put their positive attitude and high energy on display each day?

2. How could you insert joy and fun into some aspect of your job tomorrow?
3. Do you believe that the qualities of an Energizer can positively impact student learning including test scores? Why or why not?

## We Dare You Challenge

Let's suppose you would describe yourself as something like "pretty positive overall." Like many staff, you believe you are mostly positive about many aspects of your job nearly every day. Take a few minutes to focus in on one specific part of your job that you don't care for, the one you've either kept inside or expressed a somewhat negative attitude about in the past to colleagues. It's ok. We all have one. Write it down below.

_____

_____

_____

Now, shift your thinking and more importantly your words and actions from today forward. What will you do differently to turn that negative more toward a positive? Write it down below.

_____

_____

_____

Now, imagine if you actually did this (just writing it down is the easy part) and stuck to it. Imagine the increased ENERGY you'd have to put toward the aspects of your job that you do love!

## Now What?/Action Steps

If this is your CORE, you should use it for the following actions:

- Intentionally choose a positive attitude every day
- Model fun, creativity, and risk-taking for others
- Halt toxic conversations, then put them in reverse
- Achieve more by relieving pressure and stressors with FUN

## Chapter 7

### Why Every Team Needs Someone with the Energizer CORE

- To create the positive environment we all want to work in
- To be a resource to find ways to make lessons more fun and engaging
- To help the negative person see the brighter side of things
- To bring joy to otherwise-less-than-joyful tasks
- To increase the probability of positive results

### How Identifying People with the Energizer CORE Helps My School Leader

- Fun sparks creativity and increases work productivity
- Improves overall school culture
- Positive people help stop and reverse negative conversations
- There's no reason school should not be FUN

### How Understanding the Energizer CORE Helps Me Understand My Colleagues

- They are happy because they choose to be
- They know that if you stay positive in your job = you stay happy in your life
- They actually get more output from kids because of their positive attitude
- This is why kids and staff are naturally drawn to them
- They are less affected by challenges by choosing to focus on the positive

*Chapter 8*

# Helper

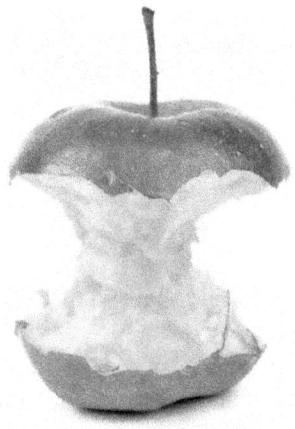

**Helper:** serves the needs of others before all else.

*There is no exercise better for the heart than reaching down and lifting people up.*

—*John Holmes*

128                    *Chapter 8*

*Gary (left): Happy birthday, brother. Another year older . . . Wait, what's with this paper looking thing wrapped around the cupcake? Maybe if I stare at it, it will magically go away.*
*Greg (right): Yeah, how's a kid supposed to eat this? What if I try to grab it from the top like this? It seems to work when I eat goldfish.*
*Both: MOM! . . . HELP!!!*

## PERSONAL STORY

The act of helping shows itself in many forms. In the vast majority of situations, it can be obvious and with only good intentions. In a few others, however, it can be hidden behind other, darker motives. This personal story is one of the latter.

Our older brother Jeff (again, it's Jeff. Man, he did a number on us, didn't he?) felt personally compelled to teach us life lessons. One would think at first glance that as his younger brothers we'd appreciate this trait. However, we're far enough into the book now that not only do you know there's way more to the story, but you're also likely thankful that he wasn't YOUR big brother.

We've shared before that growing up we spent a lot of time outside. Most of the time we were being active, engaging in some type of sport. These outdoor activities included basketball, football, baseball, frisbee, badminton, and lawn jarts (Google it—at the time, they were the kind that had metal tips and unfortunately sometimes ended with the jart landing . . . well . . . not in the lawn). Anyways, we had a smaller yard to play these activities, not nearly large enough to really meet the needs of active boys.

To have more room, much of the time we moved our games into the street. Now, there wasn't a ton of traffic so we'd play our games until one of us saw an oncoming automobile and would yell, "CAR!" At that point, we'd all pause and quickly scurry to the side of the road until it passed so we could then resume our game.

Well, it was a special "treat" (or so we initially thought) when our brother Jeff would come out to play with us. One day, we were especially ecstatic to see him strolling out of the garage with his orange aluminum bat propped over his right shoulder. This could mean only one thing! He was going to hit us baseballs! We immediately dropped whatever (incredibly important thing) we were doing and ran to get our gloves, returning to our spots in the road. What a nice big brother, hey? Hitting baseballs to his younger brothers. Or, was he?

Jeff stood in the middle of the street at the end of our driveway, ready to hit balls down the road. Since we were playing on a narrow street, we'd take turns playing infield or outfield, one of us playing directly behind the other. Right off of the road were our neighbor's driveways and front lawns that gradually sloped upward, toward their houses. The homes in the neighborhood also had shallow ditches and sewer drains just before the road. With homes fairly close to one another, we were placed three or four homes down from where Jeff was standing. You'll see why it's so important to paint such a detailed picture in a moment.

Jeff started out easy, peppering the infielder with some manageable ground balls and the outfielder with some routine fly balls. Nothing that would make us move very much. You see, Jeff had amazing control of where he hit the ball. He could hit it directly at us every single time . . . if he chose to. But alas (yeah, we used the word "alas"), he did not always choose to. You see, his motives weren't quite what we'll describe later in this chapter as the genuine "Helper" that you'd anticipate in an opening story. If this were literally any other person in the world, yes. However, after all, this was the one and only, Jeff.

Catching these initial routine grounders and fly balls made our confidence grow. Being eleven or so at the time, we'd start to believe that we were pretty good fielders and we'd inevitably develop an overly confident strut as we easily fielded the hits and threw the ball back to our big brother. Major league baseball, here we come! What we didn't know was that we were falling right into his sick, manipulative trap.

Knowing that he now had us fully trusting in him (in addition to us shouldering our inflated egos), Jeff began to waiver a little away from hitting directly to us. Once every few hits, he'd send one "accidentally" a little off the mark. No worries, we got this. We'd take a few steps away from the center of the street to snatch up that "errant" hit. After all, we were all-stars now. Nothing could get by us.

Well, little did we know at the time, Jeff was about to exploit that trust and overconfidence that he had intentionally created. Again though, we'd never realize this in the moment. It was always later and we never seemed to retain the lesson learned. This enabled Jeff to return to this "game" time and time again, year after year. That will make more sense in about twenty-one seconds.

So, these "errant" hits were not so errant at all. They were very intentional. What he'd do is start hitting these balls to places that were unsafe for our well-being . . . and all for his own twisted amusement. What would happen is that Jeff would hit high, towering fly balls that would drift over well into the different neighbors' yards. Well, how could this be amusing or entertaining to Jeff? You see, these yards all possessed different "land mines" or obstacles that could injure and embarrass us. Two outcomes that our older brother lived for.

While tracking a fly ball, we'd wander into a neighbor's yard where one of many things could result. . . . One, catch the ball and throw it back to Jeff (*great for us, but not so much for Jeff*). Two, slide/slip on loose gravel as we sprinted toward a line drive that was hit just out of our reach (*not the end of the world for us, but amusing for Jeff to watch*). Three, run into parked cars on the road or in a driveway at full speed (*Accidental? We think not*).

And Jeff's most favorite outcome of all . . . wait for it . . . he lived for this one . . . hitting it in just the right spot to lead us to a full sprint and dive into the yard of a neighbor who owned a large German Shepherd. I think you know what's coming here. It has far less to do with "helping" his little brothers improve their baseball skills than you think. A carefully placed hit would force us to dive headfirst into fresh, soft, dog poop. That's right, we'd dive after the ball and emerge streaked with dog feces on our bare legs, arms, and sometimes face. Gross, yes, and we apologize for not warning you should you be reading this while eating a snack, especially a candy bar. And yet, even before we could stand up and recognize what he had done to us . . . even before we could scream and yell and go running to the hose to wash off or into the house to tell mom . . . Jeff would have already flipped that orange, aluminum bat back over his shoulder, and calmly strolled back into the house . . . with a satisfied smirk on his face.

Now, Jeff may have come out to hit baseballs to us with seemingly good intentions. Intentions that appeared to HELP us. But, now thirty-five years later, we know that it was to HELP only one person, himself. So, "thanks" a lot Jeff, for "helping" us hone our baseball skills. Or, shall we say, "you're welcome" for helping you entertain yourself on those warm, "dog" days of summer.

## HELPER DEFINED

We define a person who is strong in the Helper CORE as someone who "serves the needs of others before all else." Like all other COREs, these characteristics in the actual definition come naturally to the Helper. It's how they view the world. It drives how they both prepare and respond to things. We submit that every single educator has Helper characteristics. If you didn't, you wouldn't have signed up for this gig in the first place. However, those with the Helper at their CORE are "next level" (pretty hip slang for a couple of forty-something-year-olds).

**Helpers' main purpose, personally and professionally, is to selflessly assist others.** They are the people we all know who seem to have extra time and energy to give to others. We see them constantly going above and beyond to help others in ways that we can't comprehend. In ways that we would have never thought of ourselves. It's not something non-Helpers should feel bad about. Remember—we're all Helpers to an extent. The Helper just naturally thinks this way. As a matter of fact, the idea mentioned earlier about how Helpers "go above and beyond" doesn't even make sense to them. To the Helper, **they're not doing anything extra, they're simply doing what's needed.**

For the Helper, perhaps as much as any other CORE, it's about other people. Whether it's in fellow staff members, students, or other stakeholders, Helpers take action to get the job done. We believe that the CORE of the Helper can best be further defined by breaking our definition down into four main subcategories as outlined below:

- Serves Others First
- Takes Action
- Understands that Kindness Costs Nothing
- Acts as a Bridge to a Goal

Read on for some related research, personal stories and next steps for you as an educator (and we promise, no more stories about dog poop.)

## SERVES OTHERS FIRST

Of all of the COREs, it's possible that the Helper and Character-Builder COREs see the big picture of life more clearly than all others. We believe that all educators go into education to help develop better people, over better learners. However, we also believe, as mentioned earlier in this book, that many of us drift away from our original values and struggle to stay true to ourselves. Instead, we are influenced by other people, as well as other things, like pressures to always be increasing the almighty student achievement data. **Successful Helpers, however, are able to stay steadfast in their initial, core values and focus on fulfilling the needs of other people first**. For the Helper, it's ALL about serving others.

**A service driven life is a significant life.** Sounds so simple, but think about it. At the end of the day, or the end of your life, don't you want to be remembered as someone who served others? Don't you want to be thought of as someone who selflessly gave of themselves so others could benefit? Don't you want others to feel that certain way about you to where the first thing they think about when you enter their mind is how you were on earth beyond all else to make life better for others? These are several deep, potentially emotional, questions. Do yourself a favor and reflect now on how others would answer those questions on your behalf thus far in your life.

In schools, we know that Helpers come in many forms. Like all of the other COREs, **Helpers can be absolutely any staff member.** Think about the people who work in your school. There are some who do their job, others who do their job well, and still others who not only do their job well but also find a way to regularly lend a helping hand to colleagues (including you) along the way. No matter if they're a custodian, an assistant or a leader, they're always serving others. Speaking of leaders, "Servant-leaders know that it is not about themselves, it is about others. And serving others . . . is not just one more item on the daily to-do list. It is what life is about. It is why we are here. It is what gives life meaning and significance" (Keith, 2011). Although Keith writes through a leadership lens, the statement is true for all staff members.

| | |
|---|---|
| | Educator: Think of your colleague who "embodies the belief that serving others gives life meaning and significance." Then, write a personal note to them recognizing them for it. |
| | Leader: Think of the staff member who you believe is strong in the Helper CORE. When assigning duties for next year like arrival or dismissal supervision or that extra study hall, instead consider leveraging their Helper CORE strength with a duty that would have a greater impact on kids. |

**Helpers don't think less of themselves; they think of themselves less.** Here's a story about just that. And, if you have a high schooler or teach high school yourself, perhaps one you'd like to share it with them to help them understand how good they've got it.

Our high school is filled with intelligent, creative, resilient and gritty kids. It's also filled with a lot of kids living in poverty. When I became principal, there was a relatively small cabinet where we kept clothes and hygiene products for kids that needed it. It was a nice way to get students a few of the basic items they needed to help them stay warm and clean. When we eventually moved into a larger building, we realized that we had more space to expand those services. The other driving force was that there was an increasing student need. Like many schools across the country, we were seeing more students without stable housing, not enough to eat, no way of cleaning themselves or their clothes, and so on.

In just over a year, and with the help of multiple staff who have Helper at their CORE, we made several additions to these services to meet the basic needs of our students. The first is, since we noticed many students often wore the same dirty clothes almost every day, we got a washer and dryer for them to wash their clothes in. It provided a free way to keep their clothes clean, while also teaching a valuable life skill.

We also stocked up on hygiene products and made it known that students could shower at school whenever they needed to. This provided a needed service to students who may have had running water for cooking or washing dishes, but not a functioning bathtub or shower. It was also useful to students who stayed at the homes of friends or extended family and did not want to use their hot water for showering. Imagine the stress relief kids who took advantage of these services felt when they knew they could come to school feeling clean and refreshed. Imagine also how learning was then made possible because of this. And, as we said at the beginning of the story, maybe, just maybe, the high schooler in your own home will be more thankful with how good they've got it as they read on.

Our staff Helpers also set up opportunities for students to receive free dental care, mental health services, and haircuts, all at school. You may have to reread that sentence to help it sink in. For kids who have rarely or never been to the dentist, a free teeth cleaning was something they didn't think was possible. For the rest of us reading this book who don't like going to the dentist at all, this puts some perspective on it, doesn't it? (We're not saying you should add your dentist to your Christmas card list, but at the very least next time you go, be more appreciative of the service that others don't have the means to receive.)

Back to the story. Obtaining mental health services in and around Milwaukee, like many places around the country, is a challenging task. This is even more difficult for parents who struggle to navigate the system, have transportation problems, or battle mental health issues themselves. So we brought the services, via outside professional therapists, to the students and families. Finally, there's not many things that can make you feel better than a fresh haircut (maybe a bit of an exaggeration, but you get the idea). Our Helpers partnered with a local barber who comes to our school twice per month and provides free haircuts (and mentoring) to our students. We set things up like a real shop, complete with a barber's chair!

And, here's the coolest example of staff serving others first. The biggest change that staff Helpers made to our school was to take that small cabinet with extra clothes and hygiene products mentioned earlier and expanded it into a 400-square foot clothing closet! The space was an old locker room that we transformed into what some students and visitors refer to as "a real store." We obtained ten clothing racks from a large retail store that had gone out of business, ran multiple clothing drives, and got donations of hygiene products from some extreme couponers. Now, students can come to the "Community Closet" and discreetly shop for free clothes, shoes, and other necessary items.

This story warms your heart, right? While it may or may not be the kind of "helping" that fits the needs of the students in your school, we'd suggest that there are unmet needs of some kind for students in every school. Yes, school is about learning, but you have to be fully prepared to receive the learning. **Helping students meet their basic needs first unlocks the doors to academic achievement**. Think about it. What unmet needs exist for the students in your classroom or school? How could you help meet them?

## TAKES ACTION

Helpers take action. They don't sit on the sidelines and wait for others. Helpers don't look around to see who will do something about it. Instead, **Helpers wholeheartedly believe that they can make change themselves.** Yes, they are the "be the change you wish to see in the world" people (Gandhi). They believe in the power of one. They are the ones who tear up when they think about the "Starfish Poem" by Loren Eiseley. You know, the one where a man encounters a young boy throwing starfish back into the ocean after they've been washed up with the tide. The beach is full of miles of starfish and the man challenges the boy's actions by stating that he can't possibly make a difference. The boy then throws one into the ocean and states, "It made a difference for that one."

> I feel so blessed to be able to help my young friends *(students)* realize their potential and feel amazing about themselves, as they should. (Laura, special education assistant)

As we stated earlier, Helpers are service driven. They live to serve others through taking action in response to their observations. "Real servants pay attention to needs. Servants are always on the lookout for ways to help others. When they see a need, they seize the moment to meet it" (Warren, 2002). Helpers act. They see a need and they act. Pretty simple. Like the

Character-Builder, they possess a whole child view of the world. **Helpers naturally look beyond the student and consider the needs of the person.** Then, they act.

Educator: Even if you don't think that you possess the characteristics of a "servant," go to school tomorrow and help a student in a way you previously wouldn't have. Be intentional about choosing the student and the act.

Leader: Pick a staff member who you feel is struggling right now. Cover their duty tomorrow, and maybe for the rest of the week or longer. Don't feel like you need to give them much of a reason. Just help them.

Here's a story about helping others by taking action. It was my first day on the job at my very first principal position. It was in an urban, elementary school of just over 600 students. If I'm being honest, I had no idea what I was doing. Full disclosure, it took me a couple of years to figure (most of) it out.

I knew after several years of teaching that I wanted to someday lead a school. However, on that very first day sitting in my office in the beginning of the summer, I wasn't sure how I got there. I knew I had to take action, but didn't know where to start. I sat alone with only two custodians in the building, with the administrative assistant enjoying a much deserved break for most of the summer. As an important aside, the previous principal was nowhere to be found, and the one brief conversation we had was, to put it nicely, not as helpful as I needed it to be. Not knowing where to start, I began on that first day by creating a task list, a "to-do" list of sorts. Things on the list included:

- Look through my office cabinets and files to see if they offered any clues
- Reach out to my elementary principal colleagues for their advice and support
- Contact and meet with the Parent-Teacher Organization (PTO) president (after determining who in the world she was)
- Figure out who the teachers and other staff members were at the school and make an initial contact.
- Get familiar with the school (translation: walk around aimlessly until I bumped into something of interest or noteworthy).

It was on that first walk, just before lunch, that I had a conversation with Jim, the head custodian. There was also a second custodian working, along with two other people who appeared to be high school students who I assumed were working there for a summer job. I watched the four of them scrub desks, clean lockers, wipe down countertops, and so on. During the conversation, I had an idea. I was excited. After all, it was my first actual idea as a principal. I decided that my first action as principal was to help, to serve alongside them doing the very work I just mentioned.

The next day I showed up in some very un-principal-like (yeah, that's a word) clothes, and got to work under his direction doing essentially the same kinds of tasks as I had observed the previous day. The two high school students looked at me like I was some kind of a nutjob. After all, who would elect to do this work when they could be doing, ummm, errrrrr, whatever it is a principal does? The two custodians pretty much had the same look on their faces.

I learned several valuable lessons by the end of that day. One was to take a pain reliever before starting a day filled with manual labor. The other was a lesson that the Helper knows ever so well, about the innate power of helping others. That is that actions speak louder than words. What I know now, and knew soon after the experience, is that working alongside those custodians and high school students made me a better person than I was the day prior. Why? Simply because my actions helped others. So, yeah, I was a Helper on that day, and hopefully many days following.

How are your daily actions in your job in education helping others?

## UNDERSTANDS THAT KINDNESS COSTS NOTHING

Helpers help because they are kind. They also understand that there is no cost to helping others. That reminds us of this famous song "Help" by the Beetles. The song is about growing into being able to ask for help from others. Ok. Admittedly, that's a strange way to open this section (or any section) of this book (or any book). But, stay with us. John, Paul, George, and Ringo had it right many years ago! I'm not sure if they had this book in mind when they wrote the lyrics, but it works, at least enough to connect those strong in the Helper CORE to kindness.

Simply put, **you must be kind to be a Helper**. Have you seen any mean Helpers out there? Didn't think so. Yeah, helping and kindness sort of go hand in hand. The same way the Energizers bring enthusiasm and positivity to everything they do, the Helpers bring kindness. It's just who they are. Helpers are genuine and caring people. They have big hearts and are constantly doing things that others see as warm and loving. To the Helper, however, they're just being themselves.

Helpers leverage what they do to change who they are, and how deeply they impact others. "Truly, the question deserving of deep reflection for us adults, then, is not 'what do you want to be?' or 'what do you do?' but rather '**who** do you want to be?' And how can what you do create a better version of who you can be?" (Schroeder, 2017) **Helpers seriously consider who they want to be and take strategic actions to get there.** Dr. Schroeder did that himself when he was the superintendent of a district when Gary was an elementary school principal. Here's your much deserved "shout out" Joe! Along the way and as an intentional result, kind acts of the Helper positively impact others. Like Joe.

Educator: No matter what grade level or department you work in, incorporate kindness into your next lesson or interaction. It can be done. Pay close attention to how people respond to you, and each other.

Leader: Assign a week at your school that focuses on kindness. Ask teachers and students (especially students, if possible) to plan it. You'll find that there are so many people ready to jump at the chance to create kindness for others, as well as so many more who desperately need it.

Helpers realize that doing the right or kind thing is not always the same as doing the easy thing. Here's a story about that from a colleague.

A SSW in an elementary school in the district where I work was serving a family who had children with attendance issues. Part of her role as the social worker was to flag "high flyers" for truancy, talk with the students, contact the family, conduct a parent meeting, identify barriers to attendance and work to remove those barriers (not easy stuff). The first step, meeting with the students, often ended up being challenging because the students were oftentimes not in school. In this particular instance, after days of trying, the students were present and an initial meeting occurred. The three children were guarded at first, but became more comfortable and slowly revealed their personalities. All three were bright, creative, and energetic. They stated that their attendance issues stemmed from their mother working odd hours and not having a dependable car to get them to school.

Meeting with the mother would prove to be even more difficult. After multiple unreturned phone calls, a letter was sent to the home explaining that if contact was not made to school, a home visit would need to occur to conduct the meeting. (Sidenote: it's an old social worker trick to get parents to reply to calls or letters. Most parents don't want someone coming to their home so they'll often reply to a school contact if they think that someone might show up on their doorstep . . . whatever works right?)

Anyways, the mother replied to the letter and a meeting at school was set. The parent arrived and was polite, but not surprisingly guarded throughout the meeting. She shared the issues she had with her work hours as well as unreliable transportation and promised to do her best to get the kids to school. Over time, the parent opened up more and began to trust the social worker. This occurred due to the social worker responding to phone calls, making positive contacts home when she noticed an improvement in attendance, helping to get them all the fixings for a Thanksgiving meal from a local church, and even signing the kids up to receive Christmas presents from the children's hospital in the city. Essentially, she was being kind. A Helper.

Things were going great until the kids suddenly stopped coming to school. The mother's phone had been shut off and she was not responding to emails or letters. The social worker conducted an unannounced home visit and found the mother and kids at home. The mother seemed distraught, but at the same time oddly relieved to see her. Through the slightly cracked open door, she shared that her boyfriend had been verbally and physically abusive to her and that she was leaving with the kids later that day. She had been in contact with a social services agency and they had found her a temporary place to stay for a few days. It was in that moment that the social worker better understood why the students had not recently been attending school, and she vowed to somehow do even more.

Over the next few weeks, the social worker stayed in almost daily contact with the mother, working to get her a more long-term solution for housing near school. Once that was secured, the last hurdle was finding furniture and appliances for her new apartment.

She enlisted the help of school staff and community businesses to acquire slightly used beds, living room furniture, a refrigerator, and a stove for the family. Everything came together on a cold Saturday in February when teachers and some of their spouses pulled up in a rented moving van to deliver the needed items. They, I mean we, were all helpers that day. I say "we," because that dedicated social worker was my wife, Jaime. She is a Helper (and an Advocate too) through and through and I'm proud to be her husband. She, and so many others, put kindness first in everything they do.

> I always strive to be that special person for students by understanding who they are, what they need as a person and a student, and how I can help them achieve. (Laura, middle school teacher)

## ACTS AS A BRIDGE TO A GOAL

A bridge is "a structure built to span physical obstacles without closing the way underneath . . . for the purpose of providing passage over the obstacle."

A person who is a bridge builder is someone who connects people despite certain differences of opinion, helping them to focus on and build from areas of agreement. An educator strong in the Helper CORE does both. Not only do they "close the (physical) way" between a task undone and one that is completed by taking action, they also build conversations up from areas of agreement so that others too feel compelled to take action.

In his book, "The Purpose Driven Life," Rick Warren writes, "Great opportunities often disguise themselves in small tasks. The little things in life determine the big things . . . Servants finish their tasks, fulfill their responsibilities, keep their promises, and complete their commitments" (2002).

For servants, or Helpers, it's not merely about providing for an individual need. It's more about providing what is needed as the means to reach a larger goal. For example, in the last story, you may have finished it smiling and feeling like the staff who participated should feel good about themselves. This is true. However, the main purpose, and Helpers know this, is to assist so as to increase the chances of achieving a larger goal. In this case, that meant getting the family stabilized so the students could have regular school attendance. Then, this school attendance would lead to increasing their knowledge and skill set, which would increase their potential for being successful later in life.

We as educators know that we can do magical things with students academically if we can get them in school every day. That's what this story was really about. About bridging the gap not about school attendance, but rather about taking care of underlying issues that were at the foundation of the kids missing school, so that they could then regularly attend school and learn. Then, and only then, are they more likely to be able to have a productive, meaningful, and happy life into their own adult years.

**Sometimes, the easiest way for people to act as a bridge to a goal is to listen.** Any counselor will tell you that some of the most impactful discussions they have had involved very little talking on their part. The success was due to listening. Do you want to help someone, but are uncomfortable or unsure of how you could possibly help? **Listen. Just listen.** Listening typically ends up revealing the real problem. A great counseling technique when someone stops talking is to simply respond with, *"And then what?"* or *"What else do you have to say?"* or *"Tell me more about that."* It keeps the person talking, gets the surface level issues out of the way and drills down to the real issues.

When I was supervising graduate-level school counseling students, the main issue they had (and I had when I began in the field) was talking too much and asking too many questions. During their time under my supervision, I'd share with them what I learned over the years. I would sum it up by telling them to *"Shut up and listen"* to their clients (students or parents, in this case). I wasn't trying to sound harsh, but rather to send a clear message that **if you want to help someone, you have to let them help themselves**. You're not typically there to give them advice. Instead, you're there to guide them to find the right answer for themselves. So, if you want a starting point to helping someone, try listening. That could very well be your first step to building a bridge between them and you and, more importantly, between them and the issue they are seeking to resolve.

Regardless of your role in education, you have many opportunities to act as a bridge to a goal. Think about that for a moment specific to your work for kids. Who do you act as a bridge for? How? When? By doing what? While the next story is about the elementary principal as a bridge builder and helper with the PTO, consider your own role and potential story as you read.

Let's begin with the common understanding that, when the PTO approaches the principal and asks for some help motivating the kids to earn money toward a fundraising goal, the principal doesn't typically say *"No thanks"* (unless they want to blow up on Twitter; it's the days we live in). The principal does typically say *"I'd love to!"* (perhaps partially because they know the alternative).

The PTO had an idea for how "we" (meaning the principal of the adjoining middle school, Mr. Petersen, and myself) could motivate the kids to raise money. Naturally, the first thing on their minds was . . . a sumo wrestling match! Of course. In my mind, I wondered what was wrong with a bake sale, spirit wear collection, Box Tops challenge, maybe even a good old-fashioned pie in the face. So, what did I say? You got it, *"I'd love to!"* Truth be told, the middle school principal and I, though he had only been there for several months, had developed a strong friendship, one that still exists today. So, essentially, let the smack talk, I mean match, begin!

We spent a few months talking up the big match on the announcements, having students make posters for the hallway of the competition including who they thought was going to win (me, obviously), contacting the local paper and closely monitoring the total money coming in. In the end, the students in both schools not only met the goal (though I think most just wanted to see two principals sumo wrestle), they actually crushed it. Crushing it was what I was going to do to Mr. Petersen. You know, to be "helpful" for the PTO.

And, well, that's exactly what happened. The day of the big match arrived. He and I spent the lunch hour wearing incredibly hot sumo wrestling suits, sweating like never before. We wanted to get the students pumped up to attend the event that was scheduled for that evening. And, attend they did. While the details of the match are somewhat unimportant (after all, we were just trying to "help" the PTO raise funds), a pummeling occurred that night. Mr. Petersen was on the receiving end of a very lopsided match.

To this day, he has a different recollection of what happened, and still debates who won. It might be because of the repeated blows he took to the head. Regardless, I remember the students chanting "Mr. Goelz, Mr. Goelz!" over and over again, as my arm was raised in victory. So, we helped out the PTO, and I got myself a (partially accurate) story for a book. Mr. Petersen, well, I think he's still in the hospital recovering.

So, what did you learn in this section about the Helper as acting as a bridge toward a goal? Three things, we hope:

1. Listen.
2. Helpers act as a bridge both by taking action and encouraging others to do the same.
3. Mr. Petersen couldn't sumo wrestle his way out of a paper bag.

## SUMMARY

*Only a life lived for others is a life worthwhile.*

—Albert Einstein

Think about this quote for a minute. Now consider the subsections of this chapter, which were how staff with the Helper CORE:

- Serve Others First
- Take Action
- Understand that Kindness Costs Nothing
- Act as a Bridge to a Goal

We hope you enjoyed the research around the topic, our own personal stories and quotes from other educators, and, perhaps most importantly, how you can activate the Helper inside of you or simply better recognize your colleagues who are strong in this CORE.

You learned that Helpers think of themselves less. That Helpers believe their purpose is to selflessly assist others. That they don't believe they're doing something extra, but rather simply doing what is needed. Finally, you learned that Helpers understand that, by meeting students basic needs first, those same students will be able to find success academically and, more importantly, beyond the school environment. It seems only fitting to bring it right back to the Beatles reference from earlier. This time, think of the student you know who needs help. Well, what are you waiting for? Don't make me come over there with my sumo suit on . . .

## Perspective-Taking Scenario

You are a seasoned veteran on your school's teaching staff. For years, you've provided high-quality instruction for students, personalized their learning, and all in all been a great teacher. Others would agree. Administration has hired a brand new teacher this year, fresh out of college.

You notice over the course of the year that she is quite comfortable volunteering for various committees and tasks that need to get done to help the department or school. You know she is also working hard for the students in her classroom and seems to be doing well, but wonder how she has time for it all, especially as a new teacher.

You conclude that she is helping out so much because she is trying to make friends with other colleagues and make sure they know she can be a team player. Probably a good move. Also, she is on Summary year this year for the evaluation cycle. So there's that. Again, good move. Smart kid. Next year, you believe she'll turn down the helping piece a little.

When the next year rolls around, she doesn't turn it down. In fact, she turns it up. She helps out even more than she did the previous year. A colleague who you know fairly well comes up to you after a meeting where this now-second-year teacher has once again volunteered for a committee and says, "*Wow, what's with _____? Is she trying to score points with the principal? She's not even up for evaluation this year. Shouldn't she be focusing more on her classroom as a newer teacher? How does she have time for all of this extra stuff?*"

How do you respond with your words? How do you respond with your actions?

## CORE Questions to Consider

1. When was the last time you "served the needs of others before all else" for a colleague? Is there a colleague right now who could use your help?
2. If Helpers are typically doing all kinds of jobs to assist others for the overall good of the school, how are they really impacting student learning?
3. Is the Helper a leader or a follower?

## We Dare You Challenge

Volunteer to help with something you normally wouldn't.
After the experience, reflect on:

- What did you put in?
- What did you get out?

PS: Gary's wife, who is a teacher, recently volunteered to serve lunch for the students at her elementary school when they were understaffed one day. She said it was the *"best part of my day."* Why do we share this brief story? Two reasons:

1. It's a practical, simple example of her taking the "We Dare You Challenge" seriously. So can you.
2. He doesn't want to get in trouble with his wife because his twin brother shared a Helper story about his own wife and he didn't. Translation: sleeping on the couch hurts his back.

## Now What?/Action Steps

If this is your CORE, you should use it for the following actions:

- Look beyond academic needs to actually improve academics
- Constantly be on the lookout for ways to serve others
- When you see a need, take immediate action
- Put others first as a way of life
- Volunteer for tasks that may or may not be directly related to your "job"

Why Every Team Needs Someone with the Helper CORE

- To display how selfless acts are contagious
- To be an active participant in the work that needs to be done
- To have someone who doesn't need the credit
- To be a listener more than a talker

How Identifying People with the Helper CORE Helps My School Leader

- Have a go-getter who is constantly thinking of others first
- Helps keep the work moving

- They're great for staff morale
- They're "go-to" people when action needs to be taken

How Understanding the Helper CORE Helps Me Understand My Colleagues

- Someone who is always helping is doing it for one reason: to achieve goals
- They don't want to lead by telling; they want to lead by doing
- Comfortable in their role as a worker, not a formal leader
- A Helper just wants to serve

*Chapter 9*

# Innovator

**Innovator:** fearlessly creates and accomplishes the unimaginable.

*Some men look at things the way they are and ask why? I dream of things that are not and ask why not?*

—Robert Kennedy

**Growing up was tough for us. We had to build with cans from the kitchen cabinet since we had no toys to play with. Early signs of future Innovators? (Note to the reader: we also had to walk to school, uphill both ways in the snow.)**

## PERSONAL STORY

"Innovators can activate both fun and fear (this will make more sense in a second) in others, at the same time." We quoted ourselves here as we use this line in the next section. Not sure how you can quote yourself before it was even written, but this book is different, if you haven't already noticed. This personal story from growing up is a perfect example of an innovator who creates fun . . . and fear, in others.

Let's get right to it in this story. In yet another attempt to amuse himself while our parents were away, our older brother Jeff decided that it would be a perfectly sensible idea to build a boxing ring in our basement for his ten-year-old brothers. Our basement was nothing special. Cement walls and a concrete floor. My parents threw some indoor/outdoor carpeting down and it housed the family's pool table, ping pong table, board games, a couch or two, and a storage area. Again, typical basement back in the 1980s (translation: no eighty-inch TV mounted on the wall with movie theater seating).

Well, where we saw a "typical basement," Jeff saw endless possibilities. In this case, a boxing ring. One day, we sat on the couches watching him use thick rope he had got from the garage and strung it around the steel support poles. At the time, we had no idea what he had in store for us.

Once this was complete, Jeff disappeared into the storage part of the basement and returned with two pairs of our father's snow shoveling gloves, mittens really. He threw them on our laps and directed us to stand up and put them on. Still not realizing what exactly was going on, we listened to his orders, knowing the repercussions, and put on the gloves. He then lifted the ropes and told us to "enter the ring." This was our first clue as to exactly what "innovation" he had been creating.

Before we knew it, we were standing in the middle of the ring with Jeff giving us instructions. He was basically repeating what he had heard from boxing matches on TV. Pretending to be a referee, he told us to have a good, clean fight (which of course, he didn't want).

We were told to touch gloves and return to our corners. He then gave some rousing introduction of us for the nonexistent crowd and rang the bell (he used our mother's dinner bell that she used to let us know to come inside for dinner). With the sound of the bell, the match began.

We approached each other tentatively, not really wanting the brawl that Jeff was salivating for. After a minute or so of dancing around the ring avoiding contact, Jeff became frustrated. This is not what he crafted this plan for. So, he began to taunt us and say things to get us mad at each other. Finally, Greg approached Gary and delivered a left jab to the stomach. Surprised at the contact, Gary bent forward at the waist, struggling to catch his breath. Seeing his chance to continue his dominance, Greg followed moments later with a monster right-handed uppercut to Gary's jaw. It was right on the money and Gary fell to the basement floor. Now, Gary still to this day debates just how much he says was "faking it" as far as actually being hurt or not. However, wouldn't you do the same if you got rocked with several punches by your smaller twin brother?

Jeff, in pure delight, lunged in between us and stopped the fight, declaring Greg the winner and undisputed champion (of what, no one knows). As he was holding Greg's arm up to the ceiling in victory, Gary decided that the fight was not even close to over yet. Filled with anger, he attacked Greg in a rage only a highly competitive twin could understand and an unscheduled wrestling match ensued. Jeff stood there watching, giddy, knowing that his plan had actually resulted in not one, but two personal victories. He had once again manipulated his two younger brothers to do whatever he wanted them to do. As a sidenote: Gary clearly won the wrestling match. In fact, considering at that time his tendency to have a "little" trouble with self-control, it took Jeff most of what he had in him to get Gary off of Greg. No glamorous story here, just the facts.

By our definition, the Innovator "fearlessly creates and accomplishes the unimaginable." With just some rope and a couple pairs of snow shoveling gloves, Jeff created a boxing ring for his younger brothers to do the unimaginable. As usual, Gary ended up with the last laugh. Or, did Jeff?

## INNOVATOR DEFINED

Thomas Edison. Steve Jobs. The Wright Brothers. Alexander Graham Bell. All Innovators. All obsessed with **taking the world from where it was to where they believed it should be**. We define a person who is strong in the Innovator CORE as someone who "fearlessly creates and accomplishes the unimaginable." An Innovator lives by the question, "Why not?" Although, in practice, it's not as much of a question as it is the definitive statement of **"WHY NOT!"** Innovators aren't interested in tradition, rules, past practices or being politically correct. Instead, they shatter "the way we've always done it" by causing a disruption with how it could be done even though no one has gone there yet. Innovators and Changers may share some of the "Why not" philosophy, but there are clear differences.

When compared to Changers, Innovators can often feel restricted and bogged down. Changers, as you recall, want to fix or "improve current systems." **Innovators believe that it's better to think big, start fresh, and create new**. Innovators look at Changers as hesitant and somewhat conservative. Like the other COREs, when the rest of us trust in them and see their perspective, they can take us to a whole new level. With Innovators, hold on tight because you're going to be on a wild, perhaps rocky, ride. The end result, though, has the potential to blow your mind!

Innovators make wonderful, seemingly impossible ideas come to life. **Innovators can activate both fun and fear in others, at the same time**. The fun is the excitement of "creating" and "accomplishing." The fear is the "unimaginable" part of our definition. We believe that the CORE of the Innovator can best be further defined by breaking our definition down into three main subcategories as outlined below:

- DreamVentor (you heard this word here first!)
- Trailblazer
- Fails Forward

As you read this chapter, think about the Innovators in your school. How do you feel about them? Consider their value, what they bring to the school that would be absent for students without them. Take their perspective.

Doing so will help you better understand what they say and what they do, and make you more open to seeing their value moving forward. *However, run, don't walk, if they get out some rope and two pairs of snow shoveling gloves.*

## DREAMVENTOR

Ok, we're going to be completely transparent with you: we couldn't decide whether to label this subsection as "Dreamer" or "Inventor" so we combined them and created a new word! It's pretty "innovative," if you stop to think about it. **Innovators are both dreamers and inventors.** They first activate their dreamer side to come up with an idea, and then take action inventing what is necessary to accomplish that goal. Said another way, **the Innovator begins with creativity and ends with action.**

The *Dreamer* part of the DreamVentor is always thinking about what they can do that has never been done before. As is the case with real dreams, they can seem crazy and out of the blue. You know, when you wake up and think, *"Why in the world was I dreaming about that? Weird."* Well, that's what we're talking about here. They are constantly looking for what might be new and exciting in education that is just waiting to be discovered. Because of this, the Dreamer part of the Innovator needs to live in a creative mental space. **The Innovator is a dreamer who is fueled by creativity, emotion and passion.** He or she is someone who excitedly thinks "outside the box," because they don't even see the box in the first place.

Educator: When you find that student engagement in a certain lesson you used to love has dropped off significantly, scrap it. What crazy thing could you do to "hook" them right from the beginning? Keep going....

Leader: Go to your Innovator in your school or department and ask, *"If there were no barriers, what would take our school to the next level?"*

The *Inventor* part of the DreamVentor is like a brilliant scientist (who may or may not be a little crazy, but in a good way). **The "inventor" side can shift from the dreamer space to one of action.** This is where the dream becomes reality. This is where the real work is done. It is where Innovators put into action things that others think are impossible. In this space, they take that original dream, the same one that non-Innovators would dismiss as impossible, and begin to consider how to make it come true. They invent things, those same things that others eventually say, *"Why didn't I think of that?"*

Make no mistake, it's hard work being a DreamVentor. When you break down the barriers, though, you can take your dreams and invent mind-blowing, innovative solutions. Even if you don't live in the Innovator space (the authors themselves don't consider the Innovator to be their CORE), it sure was fun to visit! Now go, and do.

Before we close this subsection, let's circle back to that *Dreamer* part of DreamVentor for a moment. After all, dreams are hopefully normally a pretty happy place to be, or at the very least weird enough to make dreaming interesting. Now (stay with us here), dream about sitting on a beach, watching the sunset and considering what lies ahead in your own life. If you are an Innovator: "You are the kind of person who loves to peer over the horizon. The future fascinates you. As if it were projected on the wall, you see in detail what the future might hold, and this detailed picture keeps pulling you forward, into tomorrow" (Buckingham & Clifton, 2001). The authors describe it so well here. Innovators are absolutely, wholeheartedly fascinated by the future and what could be. They dream about it. And, not just what could happen, but what they themselves can make happen. The impossible becomes possible. Ok, now wake up from your dream. You've got more book to read!

Yeah, "DreamVentors." You heard it here first. Dreamed it. Invented it. Innovated. Like the Chia Pet, we just made the word up out of thin air (props to Chia Pet DreamVentor Joe Pedott). Unlike the Chia Pet, grass will hopefully not be growing out of this book any time soon).

## TRAILBLAZER

Part of being a trailblazer is being controversial. **You can't blaze a new trail by being the second one on it.** There will be some disruption and destruction along the way. Robert Frost said it best in the last lines from his poem, "The Road Not Taken":

*I shall be telling this with a sigh*
*Somewhere ages and ages hence:*
*Two roads diverged in a wood, and I—*
*I took the one less traveled by,*
*And that has made all the difference.*

Innovators are intrigued and motivated by going places no one else has ever gone before. To venture places that seem impossible, even unthinkable in the first place. But, **Innovators live in a world with no limits**. Every step of the way is simply a part of their journey. And, that journey that is "less traveled," typically leads to places not yet discovered. Those places end up making "all the difference" for them, and for those lucky enough to be around them.

Innovators are nontraditional thinkers who don't allow barriers to stop them from accomplishing their goals. They recognize these roadblocks, but view them as insignificant and then choose to overcome them. They are able to see ahead of the curve. Able to see into the future as to what will be needed and what is possible. **Innovators are visionaries**. We have mentioned COREs who play checkers or chess. Checker players think about their current move, while chess players anticipate their opponents next five moves and attack accordingly. **Innovators absolutely play chess.**

Where Changers challenge the status quo, Innovators blow it up. This can come off as controversial, though the Innovator is not concerned with this. They are controversial for a few reasons. First, Innovators can be seen as renegades, not interested in being team players. The truth, however, is that they just choose not to be slowed down by a group. Working alone, they can progress at a fast, steady pace that large groups or systems simply can't keep up with. They know that blazing a new trail is best done alone (or with a few others who don't ask too many questions).

A second way that Innovators can be misperceived as controversial is that it can appear that they are trailblazing for themselves only. In reality, however, Innovators are making changes to help the whole group. The last person they're likely thinking about is themselves. They are not typically interested in individual accolades, and actually are instead most driven by the internal satisfaction that comes with accomplishing a goal to help others. If you don't believe that, think about the Innovators mentioned at the beginning of this chapter: Thomas Edison, Steve Jobs, the Wright Brothers, and Alexander Graham Bell. All of their innovations were for others.

Third and lastly, Innovators can be controversial because they may come off as smarter than everyone else, as "know-it-alls" if you will. These descriptions can be somewhat true and also difficult for others to accept. Think about it. If someone came up with something new, allowed nothing to stand in their way, and accomplished that thing that no one else saw as possible, aren't they a little smarter than everyone else in some way?

| Educator: What's one area of your daily work that frustrates you? Stop putting band-aids on the problem. Instead, start over. What do you have to lose? |
|---|
| Leader: Leaders need to model risk-taking and innovation. Do so by jumping feet first into a large-scale change that you've been considering. Don't worry, your team will likely appreciate the bold move and be more likely to do something similar in their own work. |

Here's some good news: **Innovators inspire others**. It's not a focus of theirs or important to them, but it can be a positive byproduct of their work. Others witness success and desire it too. From an instructional standpoint, this can be very engaging. Innovator teachers constantly introduce students to concepts out of their comfort zone and beyond the curriculum. For teachers, the following quote should remind you of the power that you have, beyond the content that you teach: "Teachers, what really matters is not so much what students walk away with in their hands, but how many sparks you ignite in their hearts. Students want inspiration more than they want stuff. The teacher, not the content, determines whether students walk away ignited or extinguished" (Breaux & Whitaker, 2006). **Innovators trailblaze and ignite**! And, that can set the stage for others to do the same! Don't believe us? Give it a try!

> I was able to watch the enthusiasm of this group of students who were given the chance to design projects that greatly interested them. (Barb, elementary teacher)

As educators, we believe that there is at least a small part inside each of us who wants to innovate, to do something different and new to impact the kids we serve. Here's a story for you about that.

At one of the schools that I served as an elementary principal of, we had a very engaged parent population who were eager to serve in their children's classrooms. Most of that service involved being in the classroom during literacy and math times. "That makes sense," said every elementary teacher everywhere, because it's during those times that more hands are always helpful. We also had high school students come to our school after their school day was over, toward the end of the elementary school day, to help individual students who were struggling in these subject areas. I know you're sitting on the edge of your seat waiting for the innovation piece (or at least not nodding off, hopefully). Here it is!

Our school recognized that the vast majority of the parent and high school volunteers were not equipped with any of the language or strategies that all other adults (teachers and aides) in the school used to support students in literacy and math. And, when you think about it, how would they be? If a teacher showed up at your house to fix your furnace, would they be equipped with the knowledge and skills to do so? Our concern, of course, was that perhaps as a result of our helpers not being trained, that there would be a disconnect for the children they were serving. Or worse yet, teaching kids new or different strategies that weren't educationally sound. And, remember, the students they worked with were our most needy kids. It's like how the teacher would most likely blow up your furnace....

Ok, here's the innovation (for real this time).... To close this gap, the reading and math coaches started providing literacy and math training sessions for parents and high school helpers! These training sessions sometimes even included the coaches modeling these learning techniques with actual children who attended the meetings! Now I don't believe we were the first school ever to have figured this out and taken action, but I do know that no one else in our district was doing it at the time. So, we were a "fearless trailblazer" in our district. Does that still count? We think so.

As a result and to conclude, I can say that these training sessions certainly created more continuity from the instruction students were receiving from school staff with instruction they were receiving from our parent and high school volunteers. And, at the end of the day, that continuity positively impacted their learning. For any educator, trailblazer or not, that's why we get out of bed each morning.

## FAILS FORWARD

"I have not failed. I have just found 10,000 things that do not work." There's no better quote to use than this one from perhaps the most famous Innovator of all time, the brilliant Thomas Edison. In it, he essentially reminds us that even if our efforts don't initially deliver the desired results, we should find what did work, capitalize on that, and persist.

Educator Innovators fail forward. They fully realize and accept that failure is part of the process to achieve success. Innovators know that without it there can be no progress toward ultimately achieving a goal. The question is not *"Will there be failure?,"* but rather *"What will the failure be and what will it teach me so that I can improve?"* In some odd way, **Innovators are encouraged by failure.** It's invigorating to them because Innovators know that, no matter how counterproductive this may sound, **when they fail, they are one step closer to success**.

Here are some quotes from Maxwell's book *Failing Forward* (2000) to help us better understand the concept as it relates to educators you work with who are Innovators:

- "Know that you're going to make mistakes. The fellow who never makes a mistake takes his orders from one who does."
- "Wake up and realize this: Failure is simply a price we pay to achieve success."
- "Achievers are given multiple reasons to believe they are failures. But in spite of that, they persevere."

We think these quotes are quite powerful. We encourage you to reread them now, thinking about your role as an educator. When you fail, do you fail forward?

Innovators are fearless. They aren't concerned with the opinions of others, what their odds are for success or whether they are told "no." **Innovators refuse to listen to the naysayers, to become complacent or be discouraged**. They look at barriers as challenges to overcome. They view roadblocks as opportunities to problem-solve. They look at problems with no answers and solve them. They will fail. Then, they'll learn and improve.

Educator: Think of the last time you quit trying something because it wasn't working, and regretted it later. Since failure is simply a part of the journey, if you had stuck with it, where would you be right now?

Leader: Celebrate failing. That's right, I said it. Celebrate failing. Start a staff meeting with a time that you failed, sharing what you gained from the experience. Knowing that you failed forward will encourage others to do the same.

In regards to change, we know that Innovators look to wipe the slate clean and start fresh as compared to tweaking something already in existence. Their work will inevitably be something new, not refurbished from something previously used (like the Changer would do).

Marzano discusses the two types of change: which he refers to as "first- and second-order change." First-order (incremental) change deals with using an existing structure, doing more or less of something, and involving a restoration of balance. This is what the Changer CORE utilizes. Second-order "deep" change is creating a completely new way of seeing things. Second-order change requires new learning, and requires what Marzano describes as "dramatic departures from the expected." This is what the innovator does. **Second-order change is change of change**. That "change of change" requires failure, but it's what the educator does with the failure that determines potential future success.

He goes on to state, "The common human response is to address virtually all problems as though they were first-order change issues. It makes sense that we would tend to approach new problems from the perspective of our experiences-as issues that can be solved using our previous repertoire of solutions." The authors submit that the importance of any change, however, is to make the change meaningful and lasting. Essentially, it's necessary to approach the change with a different perspective (second order), oftentimes starting over as opposed to tweaking what's already there.

We've always been intrigued by those who are strong in the Innovator CORE. People who live by always thinking big, taking risks, and learning along the way. I witnessed a mind-altering experience in my last year as the department chair of the school counseling department at a comprehensive high school. It was my eighth year there and I was in graduate school, again. This time working toward earning certification to be a school- or district-level administrator. In my mind, it was to work in pupil services at the district level. As is the case in most of our lives, what we have planned out rarely plays out that way (insert Thomas Rhett's "Life Changes" song lyrics into your head now if you know them).

An opening for the principal at the district's alternative education high school came open and I applied just to gain interview experience. I went into the interviews with no expectations and nothing to lose. After all, I enjoyed my current job as a high school counselor and never really considered being a building principal. Well, four interviews later, I was sitting across the superintendent's desk being offered the job.

As described in previous chapters, I struggled with the learning curve of this new position, but the point is that the people who made the decision to give me the job were absolutely strong in the Innovator CORE. Remember, I had no building-level administrative experience up to that point. I was later told that I had the disposition the staff and students needed, along with years of experience in social work and counseling that made sense for the school population. But, there is no getting around the fact that these decision-makers went away from the norm, away from the safer choices, and took a risk on me. What they did is what Innovators do: they took a chance, and a big one at that. They were going for Marzano's "second-order" change.

The point of the story is that Innovators like the ones who hired me were willing, in some ways, to risk short-term failure for eventual, long-term success. Although they were confident that I would be successful, they knew that, even during times of failure as I learned how to lead a school, I'd be failing forward. I have, we have, and our students are better off because of it.

Think for a moment about the Innovator(s) in your building. Do they fit the components that were shared in this chapter? Now think about them some more and consider where you'd be (or where your school would be) without them. **Innovators play a key role in moving learning forward.** Trusting and embracing them will take you far. If you haven't taken the time to thank an Innovator you know, you should.

## SUMMARY

**Innovators ignite.** Do you? If so: "You are a dreamer who sees visions of what could be and who cherishes those visions. When the present proves too frustrating and the people around you too pragmatic, you conjure up visions of the future to energize you. They can energize others too" (Buckingham and Clifton). A lot of this book is not only hopefully rejuvenating for you personally as an educator to help you get back to your own CORE (purpose), but also eye-opening with regards to the necessity to appreciate the strengths your colleagues bring to school each day (perspective). This quote speaks more to the latter part, and is especially important for those strong in the Innovator CORE.

If you're naturally less inclined to innovate, no problem. However, think of the Innovators around you, and the great value they bring (even if they can seem to be a little over the top at times). I'll bet there is a part of you who admires them for "fearlessly creating and accomplishing the unimaginable." Or, at the very least, and perhaps without you even realizing it, a part that lights a small fire inside of you to try something innovative in your role. Why not give it a try, tomorrow?

We explained Innovators in this chapter in these subsections:

- DreamVentor
- Trailblazer
- Fails Forward

Before moving on, we encourage you to individually reflect or talk with a colleague about what you learned from these sections. And, more importantly, how this learning can improve what you do for kids. What actions can you now take? How can you innovate? If you don't take action, what's the point of what you just learned?

## Perspective-Taking Scenario

You're a first grade teacher. In the past couple of years, your principal has shown an interest in integrating new and innovative teaching and learning practices. In response, sixth grade teachers started having "Genius Hour." You are currently in a staff meeting that the principal is presenting at regarding this topic. He states, *"Genius Hour allows students to explore their own passions and encourages creativity in the classroom. It provides students a choice in what they learn during a set period of time during school. The sixth grade teachers provide a set amount of time per week, one hour, for the students to work on their projects. The students choose the topics themselves because it's of interest to them. They spend several weeks researching the topic before they start creating a product that will be shared with the class or school. Throughout the process the teacher facilitates the student projects to ensure that they are on task."* He goes on to give more details about the benefits of Genius Hour from his perspective.

At the end of the staff meeting (right around when all of the teachers are figuring out how they can make copies, grab more paper clips from the office, and use the bathroom all while getting back to their classrooms in three minutes), the principal drops the bomb that next year all kindergarten through fifth grade classrooms will implement Genius Hour. You're not sure that first graders can handle Genius Hour, and the principal didn't mention this being done at lower grades at other schools. You suddenly forget about most of those other tasks as you lock eyes with your grade-level colleagues and begin to walk back toward your classrooms.

- What do you do (other than go use the bathroom)?
- More importantly, what do you say?
- Essential question: Are you a fearless trailblazer willing to do something unimaginable?

## CORE Questions to Consider

1. At what age are students able to innovate? How? What does it look like?
2. If there aren't any innovation-related questions on state-mandated assessments, why are we as educators spending more time on implementing innovative teaching and learning practices in our classrooms?
3. When your students fail, what do you encourage them to do? Do you do the same when you fail? Why not?

## We Dare You Challenge

Most educators, regardless of their role, have something innovative they've seen a colleague do that would be new for them to try. Remember, you don't have to be the first one in the history of the world to do something new for it to be innovative. There is value in you being innovative for yourself. Let's call that "internal innovation." (Sidenote: if that term takes off, you heard it here first).

What is one new, innovative practice YOU could try for you, regardless of your role in schools? I know, I know, you don't have time. Make time. It's what Innovators do. Think. Think some more. Think a little more. Got it? Not yet? Grab some caffeine. Got it? Great. Go, do. I dare you. Then, more importantly, after you fail forward which leads you to eventual success, share with others.

## Now What?/Action Steps

If this is your CORE, you should use it for the following actions:

- Always look to invent new and better things
- Spend time thinking about possibilities, not limitations
- "No risk, no reward" mentality
- Spends more time looking ahead, than back

Why Every Team Needs Someone with the Innovator CORE

- To invigorate others out of stagnancy
- To be the first to try something
- To show others what can be accomplished when you think big
- To see/stay ahead of the curve

How Identifying People with the Innovator CORE Helps My School Leader

- Helps break out of the "how we've always done things" mentality
- Every school needs DreamVentors (Dreamer + Inventor)
- Pushes limits
- Models to others what is truly possible

How Understanding the Innovator CORE Helps Me Understand My Colleagues

- Starting from "square one" is just some people's default
- Some people just operate better by shaking things up and trying new things
- They're always playing chess (thinking several moves ahead)
- They require mental stimulation and challenge

*Chapter 10*

# Leader

**Leader:** creates, supports, monitors, and facilitates the work.

*Leadership is not about a title or a designation. It's about impact, influence and inspiration. Impact involves getting results, influence is about spreading the passion you have for your work, and you have to inspire teammates and customers.*

—Robin S. Sharma

162                              *Chapter 10*

**What? Did you think someone else started the "short shorts" and "knee high socks" trend? We think not. It was us! We were leading the way with that many years ago. And, these days, it's back again (though we can't take credit for it!).**

## PERSONAL STORY

We define leaders as those who "create, support, monitor, and facilitate the work." Well, we have a personal story that exhibits all of these components. And, we'll even involve our oldest brother, Mike, in this one too. As you've certainly noticed, he's not been mentioned nearly as much as Jeff in this book. However, when you think of it in terms of what light Jeff has been mentioned in, maybe that's a good thing. You're welcome, Mike.

In our family, Sundays always began with going to church. As our brothers got older and could drive, we were allowed to attend the late service, which started at noon. What started out as a cool way to spend quality time with our older brothers, whom we admired (for some odd reason), soon turned into yet another way for us to be used by them. You see, Mike and Jeff figured out a way to avoid church altogether, without getting in trouble from our parents. And it, of course, required us to go along with the plan or suffer the consequences.

Here's how Mike and Jeff "created, supported, monitored and facilitated" this work. As we left the house that first Sunday on our way to church, our brothers were all smiles, reassuring our parents that they were happy to be model older brothers. However, their smiles simultaneously turned to devious grins as they turned their backs to our parents and went to the garage to get in mom's car.

We rode in silence to church that day, until we rolled to a slow stop in front of the main entrance. This was odd. We needed to be in a parking spot to all get out of the car and attend church. Instead, both brothers turned to us and explained that we were not all going to be attending church that day, or any day in the near future, for that matter. You see, they had come up with a plan. And the plan involved throwing the frisbee around and fishing at a nearby park, not going to church.

You see, we, as the younger brothers, were charged with the act of obtaining "proof" that we had attended church. For our family, that meant returning home with a church bulletin. Well, our brothers decided that each Sunday, while they waited in the car, we would take turns walking into the church lobby, approaching an usher, smiling, taking the weekly bulletin, thanking them, then turning around and exiting the building without raising any suspicions from the usher or priest. (Of course, the Almighty knew, so we'll have to answer to Him at some point.) That's right, our trusted (sort of) brothers made us commit this act each and every Sunday. Then, we'd guiltily go to the park with them, only to return home and slide the bulletin across the kitchen counter as we walked red-faced past one of our parents hoping to God (literally) that they didn't ask what we had learned at church that day.

So, as you can see, after "creating" this plan each week, Mike and Jeff would indeed "support, monitor and facilitate" the work we were forced to complete. While admittedly not exactly what we had in mind when defining the Leader CORE, it does fit the criteria. Let's call it a "gray area," shall we? So, what happened in the end? Well, this ritual went on for months, until a neighbor who went to our church mentioned to our father that he thought it was odd that he sent his kids to church for a bulletin every week, when he could just pick it up earlier in the morning after he attended service.

This revelation resulted in a very brief, but direct, discussion between our older brothers and my father. That was followed by a swift response from our brothers toward us, because somehow them getting caught was all our fault. We won't share the details here. However, if you've been paying absolutely any attention to the treatment we received from our brothers growing up, then you have a pretty good idea about some possibilities for the rest of the story. And, as you may have guessed, from then forward, each Sunday we stayed in church longer than just to grab the bulletin.

## LEADER DEFINED

First off, we want to make it clear that this CORE has little to nothing to do with an educator's job title. After reading this chapter, we hope that the reader will fully understand that absolutely anyone who works in education, and we mean anyone, can have Leader as their CORE. Like every other CORE you have learned about, **it's about possessing the attributes described within the CORE and what you do with them, not your title**. So, aides, teachers, support staff, all educators, read this chapter closely. We guarantee that you can find a Leader in the aide who you have recess duty with, the teacher whose classroom you work in or the head custodian who does so much more than maintain the physical school building. Leaders are abundant in your school, and they're not just in the main office.

The reader needs to understand that being a formal leader per their job title does not mean that they should immediately default to thinking that the Leader is their strongest CORE. Many of the most effective leaders we know would indeed connect more with the attributes of one of the other nine COREs. We'd submit that's ok, and in many cases a good thing. In fact, the most dynamic teams we've ever been a part of, including teams from grade-level teacher teams to district office leadership teams, have most team members who are strong in other COREs like Collaborator, Energizer, Innovator, Character-Builder, or many others.

One final note as part of our definition of Leader: for the Leader to be successful in anything they do, they need trust. It's the foundation for everything else. Without it, any positive outcomes that occur are based on other factors. Think about that. **Even the best idea is often dismissed before consideration based simply on whether people trust the person having it**.

It doesn't matter how smart or articulate you are. It doesn't matter what college degree you have or your past successes. It doesn't matter if you are a nice person or liked by others. It doesn't even matter if you have an official "leader" role. All that matters is trust. If others trust you, they'll actually be listening to your idea instead of waiting for you to stop talking. Keep trust in mind as you read this chapter. When trust is present (in the classroom, in a staff meeting, at the district office, etc.), there is likely a leader experiencing success for those they lead.

We believe that the CORE of the Leader can best be further defined by breaking our definition down into three main subcategories. Warning: only one subcategory is about actual leading. That's intentional and we'll share more as we go. Here they are. The Leader:

- Leads
- Follows
- Influences

As you read this chapter, think about the leader (administrator) in your school. How do you feel about them? Consider their value, what they bring to the school that would be absent for students without them. Additionally, how has the role of leader/principal changed over time? Translation: think about your own principal from "a few" (you're welcome) years ago when you were in elementary school as compared to your current principal.

Likely, there are many differences that just popped into your head. Ponder how the official leadership role has changed over the years. Finally, think about a leader in your school who is not an administrator. What is their job title? What qualities do they possess that makes them a leader? As teenagers, did they force their younger siblings to get a church bulletin? So many, many questions.

Educator: Think about the most effective leader(s) you ever worked with. Staff trusted them, right? What specific actions did they take to earn that trust? Do you behave in the same way to earn the trust of those you lead (your students or others)?

Leader: Who is someone in your school who you would trust to lead something, yet you have not yet tapped to do so? What are you waiting for?

## LEADS

Imagine a mother duck in a pond with her ducklings swimming behind her in a straight line. The obvious question in your head right now is . . . *Why am I doing this?* (It's funny because you were actually just thinking that.) Here's the answer:

1. It's a cute visual.
2. It paints a quick picture of what a staff member strong in the Leader CORE does, at times. They're, well, out in front, ummmmmm, leading!

After all, how could we possibly have a Leader CORE and not have one of the main components be about actual leading, right? Well, the ability to lead out in front of others is in fact an attribute for Leaders and so we thought we'd start with it. While it's the most obvious characteristic of a Leader, it's one that is worthy of some consideration here.

**Leading looks different for different people and in different situations.** However, there are common themes. We think the best leaders seemingly inherently just know when to be out in front leading others and when to intentionally retreat to let others lead (more on that in the next sections). Even the strongest, most powerful leaders lose some of their influence if they choose to be up front all of the time. These leaders, and we don't care how collaborative or successful they may be, become a sort of "white noise" at some point. Innovation and progress can be stifled by leaders who always position themselves in the front. So, good leaders strike the balance, knowing when it's important to lead from the front.

**Good leaders have a pulse on when a decision is needed and act accordingly.** They can determine what others need and then deliver it to them, rather than focusing on fulfilling their own needs. In the long run, this type of approach typically yields the best results for everyone involved, including the leader. Sometimes a leader is needed in the front to provide direction.

Leaders often find success being assertive and straightforward. Again, some situations call for that. In these cases, people may need a difficult decision made or a sensitive situation confronted. This is when a leader is needed that will make the *right* decision, not the *easy* one. Leaders do not put off the issue; they swiftly assess it and react accordingly. They are committed to intentionally gathering pertinent information and then use it to make a well-informed, intelligent, and unbiased (as much as is possible) decision. Not everyone always agrees with the decisions of the leader during these times, but they are typically respected for their processes and fairness.

That said, sometimes a leader is needed as a stabilizing force, often during times of crisis. These leaders could be described as the "rock" of the school. They are the ones people are drawn to, whether they realize it or not, during confusing or tough times. When staff are searching for an explanation or to make sense of something, they go to this person. While they might not need to provide a decision right there in the moment as was described in the previous paragraph, here this person provides the support and comfort that people need. Here's a personal story about that very kind of leadership.

The Sandy Hook Elementary School shooting in 2012 was a horrific tragedy. From that awful tragedy, though, somehow came stories of hope and encouragement. This is one of those stories.

As an elementary school principal, I realized that Monday as I drove to school that today the parents and students needed a compassionate, subdued, stoic leader who was out in front. Since I wasn't sure what the students had heard or perhaps seen on TV over the weekend at home about this awful day, if anything at all, I was thinking mostly about the parents.

Sandy Hook rocked all schools (especially elementary) around the nation, as it brought home the chilling fact that "it" could happen anywhere at any school level. I wanted to personally and individually reassure each parent as they dropped off their children that morning that their child was going to be safe at school that day (and every day), just as they had been prior to Sandy Hook.

While it was typical that I'd be visible for students at the morning arrival time, normally near the main entrance doors, today was going to be different. I intentionally placed myself directly in the spot where parents pull up in their cars several at a time to drop their children off. I was, quite literally, leading from out front.

That day, to every single parent, I met them at their driver's side door. They each tentatively rolled down their car window, wondering why the principal was approaching them (and likely hoping for the best). What I did was shake their hand, look them straight in the eyes, and say something to the effect of, "Samantha is safe here at school today and every day. We'll take excellent care of her until you pick her up at the end of the day." Literal tears ran down the faces of some, others simply quietly gave me a "thank you" or didn't know what to say. The look in their eyes said it all. Although I was shaken that day myself, I recognized what others needed and gave it to them. They needed the leader to lead.

One final aspect of the "Leader" subcategory is about the Leader as a visionary. Along with providing others what they need, another common attribute of successful leaders is their ability to possess and articulate a clear vision. After all, like the mother duck referenced earlier, every organization needs to know *where* they're going. **Effective leaders have the long-term future in mind as they take tiny steps forward in the present**. Lovejoy and Stetzer wrote, "If we're not intentional about the vision, we will lose it. We will drift off course. We will end up going somewhere we don't want to go and will end up becoming something we don't want to become. We will end up wasting our time. Our organizations will cease to fulfill the purposes for which they were created" (2016).

Leaders keep a group on course. They do this by being out front at times. Again, think beyond the formal leaders in your organization. These people recognize when we may be straying from the intended outcome. They refocus our efforts back to the vision of the work and challenge us to stay committed to the task at hand. They do this in an unwavering way that gives the rest of the group the confidence and stability needed to get back on track. They see the big picture and make sure that the current work or conversation aligns with getting there.

Educator: Your current role likey sometimes requires you to be assertive and decisive. Reflect on a recent time where you were faced with a situation where you had to lead, to make a difficult decision. In that situation, who needed you to act and in what way? Do you think you fulfilled their need? What would have happened if you did not get out front and lead?

Leader: We learned in this section about leaders being out front, leading. Think of a time when you weren't out front but should have been. Why weren't you? What was the end result? What did those staff who you did not effectively lead miss out on as a result? What is your takeaway?

While it's obvious that leaders lead, it's less obvious that leaders follow. In fact, **the best leaders spend a fair amount of time following**. Aristotle said, "He who cannot be a good follower cannot be a good leader." So, if you don't trust us, trust him! He's (slightly) more intelligent than both authors (combined). So, read on!

## FOLLOWS

Back to those ducklings with their mother (you know you were hoping we'd come back to them!). After all, mother doesn't lead out in front forever. How would her ducklings ever learn to spread their wings and fly on their own if she doesn't let them get out front and try? Envision now the mother swimming in the pond but her ducklings being around her, beside her, and at times even inching out in front. The reality is, she transitions from leader to something of a follower at around month two (thank you Google for that interesting fact). Again, why do you need to know this?

1. Who doesn't need more random facts about ducks?
2. To illustrate that a leader is also a follower.
3. It's (still) a cute visual.

**The best leaders know when to follow.** We'll learn in this part of the chapter that a leader should also be a follower, someone who supports the work. As a principal, I'd like to share one example. As always, as you read, think about when you followed others, regardless of your role.

At the school where I served, we conducted classroom walkthroughs (seven- to ten-minute unannounced observations in classrooms). On occasion, I'd do these walkthroughs with the reading or math coach. During these particular walkthroughs, I was very much (and intentionally) the follower.

Since I was especially fortunate to work with exceptional reading and math coaches, taking a backseat to them was not a problem. As we'd walk through classrooms and have conversations afterward about our observations including what to offer the teacher as positives as well as next steps for their growth, the coach often drove of the conversation. Why? Frankly, because they knew as much or more (usually more) about instructional best practices across all grades in their subject than I did, and they certainly knew the curriculum better.

It was through those conversations that not only did I grow as a leader in those content areas, but the coach grew into a leader as well. I'm not sure which was more prominent or important, but I am sure of one thing . . . it doesn't matter. By me taking on more of a supportive role, I learned and became better able to provide teachers with meaningful feedback regarding their instruction when the coach (mother duck) was no longer by my side. Additionally, the coach was built up as a leader which impacted other aspects of her job. Simply put, **Leaders recognize when following is actually leading**.

We fully realize that this idea of followership completely contradicts most traditional leadership philosophies. After all, when you think of a "leader," you quite naturally think of someone who is in the front, literally, leading the charge. However, being that intentionally following is at the core of the authors leadership styles, it absolutely had to be in the book.

We like to use the term "getting out of the way" or "leading from the side." We've also discussed "knowing your role." Sometimes, even if you're a leader with the title, your role is to follow. After all, effective leaders are almost entirely successful due to the work of others. Pause to think about that in your current role. Recently, when could you have stepped aside to let your students, colleagues, or whomever, lead? How might things have gone even better had you done so?

There may be some initial risk at first of not leading in the traditional sense of the word, but good followers have the intuition and confidence to know when to step back and let others lead. There can actually be a sense of calmness in these situations when the "leader" comes to terms with the fact that others can potentially, or even certainly, do a better job at something than they can. It takes a humble "leader" to intentionally get out of the way and let others make the decisions and do the work. Leaders, it can be as simple as sitting down among the other educators in your school during a meeting that you typically lead from the front. That single act alone, following, can be a powerful force.

A powerful experience I had with recognizing the strengths of others and giving up my power took place just days into my principal position at an alternative education high school. When I took the position, I did what a lot of principals do in a new building, I drafted a letter to staff to introduce myself and offer them an opportunity to meet with me. One particular staff person met with me and quickly got to something they were very passionate about. The teacher shared with me that over the years the staff themselves had taken on an active role in decision-making.

The veteran teacher shared with me that one key component to their school structure was a weekly, teacher-led staff meeting, of which building administrators did not participate. To this day, I am uncertain whether the previous administrator implemented this practice or whether the staff used their assertiveness to make this happen. Either way, who was I to get in the way of a traditional staff practice in a new building? Oh yeah, I was the principal.

So many of you are probably thinking, *why didn't you stop this? It's your job to assess these things and determine whether to allow them to continue or not. What if the teachers just complain at all of these meetings about the administration?* Point taken. Full disclosure: it was my first building leadership position and I lacked the confidence initially to stop this, or to know that I could even consider doing so.

Looking back, I'm thankful now that in this instance I followed. I'm glad I didn't end the practice. I took the risk and gave up my power to allow (and later, encourage) this practice to continue. As mentioned previously, I was not "allowed" in these meetings. However, the teacher-leader who ran them would let me know if there were issues that the rest of the staff wanted brought to my attention. Well, let me tell you, during those first few meetings I waited nervously to see what complaints would be "brought to my attention" by the teacher-leader. What I found out over time (five years and counting) is that I was rarely, yes rarely, brought anything at all. Maybe the staff just needed a voice and others to listen to it. Hmmmmm.

The staff used the time as a safe place to run ideas past one another, collaborate as teachers, and accomplish tasks that either they identified as school needs or I passed along to them as issues to solve as a team. Risky for me? *Yes.* Empowering for staff? *Definitely.* Successful in creating systems of collaboration to accomplish goals for our school? *Absolutely.* **Sometimes,**

**following is leading** (unless your brothers tell you to sneak into church to get a bulletin).

If you're into sports (or even if you're not), think of it this way. Pick your favorite player on your favorite team and read on. A good leader (insert player name here) is seen at times as just another player on the team. They're not necessarily always acting as the coach or the team captain. The good leader can be a role player. We'd argue that the most effective leaders in schools can "blend into the woodwork." After all, the real work is done as a team. And, while that player at times "takes over" the game and/or hits the winning shot, more often than not, they're doing things to help others on the team toward the goal of winning the game.

As we close this portion of the chapter, we suggest that you rethink what you previously thought about followers. The truth is, followers are typically humble, loyal, and committed team players. We'd encourage you to help followership get rid of the "bad rap" that it currently has in some circles. After reading this portion of the chapter, you now know the truth. The truth is:

1. Any staff member can be a leader.
2. Any leader can (and should) be a follower at times.
3. Mother duck is both! (Though we'd suggest NOT calling your principal a "Mother Duck" when they step aside to follow at your next staff meeting.)

Never underestimate your impact! (Anne, elementary school instructional coach)

## INFLUENCES

This subcategory makes the most sense when approached from the standpoint of a scenario. If you were a building leader and you needed someone to lead a group of staff to complete a specific task, how would you decide on that person? Would you go with the staff person who has the most experience? Would you go with the staff person who possesses the most in-depth knowledge on the subject? Would you go with the staff person who typically agrees with you or maybe even the one that most others like? Do you feel like you're being set up right now?

Well, you are. If you want positive results, while you would consider these criteria, one not yet mentioned would likely be your best choice. If you want the best chance of success, you'd tap the staff person that has the most influence on others. **The most effective leaders are the strongest influencers.**

An educator strong in the Leader CORE influences in many ways. One way is by building and using trust (discussed earlier) to influence others. The main way leaders influence others through building trust is by keeping them feeling valued, positive and motivated. A valued staff person will feel energized to do just about anything for their leader. There are many ways to get people to feel valued, but one great way is by giving them a voice.

If you work in a school with committees (and who doesn't?), those committees should at times have free rein to develop and implement action, not just meet to create proposals of action to be delivered to the principal for his/her approval. They should have the freedom, ability, and trust to make decisions and put them into action. The story that we shared earlier in this chapter about teacher-led meetings is a perfect example of this. Building leaders need to let go and return the trust back to their staff.

Another way Leaders influence others is by creating and maintaining a positive environment. So much of this is determined by how the Leader communicates. "Remember that talking about successes makes people feel successful, whereas talking about overwhelming obstacles makes people want to give up" (Gruenert & Whitaker, 2015).

This doesn't mean that difficulties are ignored, but the successful Leader sets the tone with their attitude and communication. Positive leaders don't necessarily have schools with positive environments (yet), but we'd be hard-pressed to find an example of a school with an overtly negative leader who is able to produce a positive work environment. Think about that in your current role. *Does your leader positively influence others by what they say?* Think about that in your own classroom or work environment, where YOU are the leader. How would you answer that question for YOU? Did you like your answer?

Still another way a Leader influences is by modeling. Who wants to follow someone who wouldn't even do the things that they're asking others to do? (Unless of course that "someone" is your big brother who wouldn't get a church bulletin himself and is actually modeling what not to do.) Modeling the behavior we want to see is the easiest way to gain buy-in from others. Staff will follow someone who "walks the walk" and is right there alongside them doing the work. There is a sense of pride that Leaders feel when they are on the "front lines" of the difficult work being done in schools today. Effective leaders roll up their sleeves and join in, and others respect them for that.

The last way a Leader influences others is by motivating them. Influencers create an environment where people want to come to work and be a part of something amazing. Staff in these situations have the energy and drive to accomplish great things, things they never thought possible. Keep the Leader as motivator piece in your head as you read on.

As you know from reading about the Leader CORE thus far, a leader leads from a variety of positions. Sometimes, leaders lead from out front. Other times, they lead from alongside or from behind (follow). This story is about leading from another position . . . above. No, this is not a reference to a leader being "above" their staff. This story is about leading from above, quite literally. As in, from the roof. As you read it, think about leadership through the lens of being an influencer and a model (No, not *that* kind of model. Have you seen my picture?)

Each year, our elementary students had a big fundraiser. One particular year, the "reward" if they met their goal was for me to sleep on the roof of the school that night. In this instance, leadership was about a lot of the "little things" that would collectively make this a memorable experience for the students, one that would influence them moving forward for future fundraisers and hopefully as young people in general. So, I:

- contacted the local fire department and arranged for a truck with a huge ladder to put me on the roof that night.
- wore my pajamas to school (the one and only day I was actually comfortable in my clothes as a principal!).
- borrowed a megaphone from the phy. ed. teacher to be able to talk to the kids from the rooftop.
- tied a rope to a bucket to lower it from the rooftop so that those families who couldn't come at the exact time I was being lifted onto the roof could bring me items throughout the night and early morning hours to make my stay a little more comfortable. I know you're curious about the items they brought, but I enjoy my job too much to put them in writing.
- stayed up there until the following morning to greet the kids upon their arrival at school, so that even if they didn't attend the prior night, they'd have a special memory.
- after school started that morning, I made sure to visit each classroom, still disheveled from sleeping on the roof, to thank the kids for reaching the fundraising goal (and see if any of them had a comb or a toothbrush that I could borrow).

As we said, a leader influences in many ways. One is by modeling. Even had I not done some or any of what was mentioned above, by agreeing to sleep on the roof, I was modeling for them the importance of fundraising for our school (and as a leader to do whatever it takes) to raise money to acquire things necessary to maximize their learning. Think about it. And, if you decide to sleep on the roof, I'd suggest you bring a soft pad to sleep on and an extra pair of socks (since my back still hurts and I have yet to regain feeling in my toes from that cold March Wisconsin evening).

Influencers help those who are motivated to change generate the courage to take action. Influencers may not even truly comprehend the power that they have over others. They often do so subtly and quietly. Most others recognize their "power," but often the influencer themselves may not see it. Apply that to the mother duck (who you were secretly hoping we'd bring back). . . . She's influencing those ducklings, one little web-footed paddle at a time. Who have you lifted recently (hypothetically speaking)?

One final quote for you to consider: "Having influence is not about elevating self, but about lifting others" (Sheri Dew).

Educator: Pick a student who needs a helping hand. What is one thing you could do tomorrow to positively influence them? Go.

Leader: As a leader, you influence others. If you had to pick one person on staff who you have yet to have a significant influence on, who is it? What is one thing you could do tomorrow to influence them?

## SUMMARY

Whether you're leading the way with short shorts or socks pulled up to your knees, those educators strong in the Leader CORE possess three main attributes: Leader, Follower, and Influencer. The first one needs no review since it's what we traditionally have thought of when we think about leaders, but the other two are worth briefly coming back around to.

If you've got only one thing from this chapter, we hope that you've been able to change your perspective about the idea of who a leader is and what they do. A leader can be anyone, regardless of title. A leader can also be a Follower and an Influencer.

An effective Leader strategically follows and influences, as opposed to always being out front leading. Like the mother duck (you really didn't think you were going to get out of here without a final duck reference, did you? Last one, promise), there is a time to lead, and also a surprisingly frequent amount of time to follow and/or influence when not out front.

Moving forward, open your mind to what you learned about Leaders from this chapter. Think about both the official and the unofficial leaders in your school or district. Think about when they lead, when they follow, and when they influence. Take their perspective on things. Go ahead, take a quack (I mean crack) at it.

## Perspective-Taking Scenario

You are a staff member of many years in what you believe is overall a very good school, with equally good leadership. Your principal prides herself on being a Follower and Influencer seemingly as often as she does on being a Leader. For example, she has teachers from various departments/grade levels involved with the creation of much of the overall school schedule each year. Also, she asks that at least one staff member share a teaching best practice that they are implementing in their classroom at each staff meeting. Finally, much of the curriculum-related professional development that occurs is done so by the instructional coach or other teachers.

This year, a teacher from another school in the district transferred to your school. She has taught for thirty years, you believe she is effective, and notice she is also quite strong in her beliefs about how a school should be led. Midyear, she comes up to you asking about why the principal doesn't lead more. She states that at her previous school the principal was "in charge" of the very things described above. You used to have a principal who led in that fashion. You believe that since the current principal got the job, that you have a better schedule, have learned a lot at staff meetings from other teachers, and finally feel that the professional development you receive from coaches is the best PD you've ever been a part of. What do you say to your new colleague? Are you strong enough to **influence** her so that she **follows** your **lead**? (See what we did there, pretty fancy, right?)

## CORE Questions to Consider

1. Is a leader most effective when out front? Can they effectively lead from the shadows, or is that just plain creepy?
2. Likely, your parents would define a leader (their boss when they were in the work world) differently than you would. The role of "Leader" has changed over time. Discuss.
3. Influence is something that's difficult to quantify, but is an important part of being a leader. What influence are you having on your colleagues? How do you know?

## We Dare You Challenge

Where do you typically lead (teach) in your classroom relative to the students? In the front, right? Of course, makes sense. You don't want your students to be facing forward and not see the teacher who is talking or facilitating the conversation. **Now, can you lead your classroom from the back for a while?** Literally. Walk behind your students, assuming you have your classroom set up where that is possible. If not, simply walk to the opposite part of the room where you normally stand. See what happens. You'll find that changing your proximity to the students changes everything. You learned in this chapter that a leader doesn't have to lead from the front. In fact, you might be more effective from, well, anywhere else! And, this holds true for many other roles in education as well, not just teachers. If you're not a teacher, modify this challenge to make it fit for you. Then, try it. We dare you.

**Now What?/Action Steps**

If this is your CORE, you should use it for the following actions:

- Be confident that you know what success looks like
- Model what you want to see from others
- Take charge when necessary
- Listen

Why Every Team Needs Someone with the Leader CORE

- To accomplish things together, that individually you couldn't
- To help connect the work to the overall end goal
- To keep the team focused and on track
- To grow others in their thoughts and actions

How Identifying People with the Leader CORE Helps My School Leader

- All schools need leaders who don't necessarily have leadership in their job description
- Sometimes people listen more to leaders who are not labeled as such
- Encourages formal leaders to delegate more
- Reduces some of the administrator's workload so they can focus on other things
- Gets others to consider what they could be leading

How Understanding the Leader CORE Helps Me Understand My Colleagues

- There is a leader in everyone
- The desire to lead something does not mean that person wants to be a formal leader
- Unofficial leaders are often rejuvenating themselves in some way when they lead
- Leading can be done from out front, from the side or from behind

*Chapter 11*

# Preparer

**Preparer Defined:** connects learning to life in a way that gets students ready for their future.

*Give me six hours to chop down a tree and I will spend the first four sharpening the axe.*

—Abraham Lincoln

**Look at these outfits! Were we preparing to hit the ball or preparing to not have any friends? Gary (left), was showing so little leg that he must have been preparing for an early snowfall. Greg (right) was preparing for a "wardrobe malfunction" as he was wearing two pairs of shorts!**

## PERSONAL STORY

This personal story is more than about being prepared for the day, it's about preparing for life. We define Preparers as those who "connect learning to life in a way that gets students ready for their future." Our father, Marvin (but you can call him Marv if you like), probably didn't realize it, but he lived his life teaching his four sons the values needed to live a fulfilled life. We grew up seeing him as a hard-working, reliable, fair, and firm man. He showed these characteristics as a husband, father, coworker, friend, neighbor, and so on. As a father, the man was a rock. And, since we haven't said it enough, "thank you, dad." For all of it.

Dad would attribute these traits to his strict German upbringing. As kids growing up, we didn't know any different so we just assumed that this was how everyone's father was. Looking back, dad was meticulous and intentional in everything he did. You should have seen our lawn! The lines from the mower were perfectly straight, with the grass cut frequently and to just the right height. Although he and our mother had us doing chores and working at young ages, we were not allowed to cut the grass. That's right, with all of the work around the house to do, you'd think that our old man would make any of his four sons mow the lawn. Not this guy. He would not relinquish that task because he knew that none of us could match his attention to detail and perfection.

This perfectionist attitude was displayed in everything he did. It could be seen in his preparation for, and execution of, his morning routine, which is what this story is about. Yeah, we all have one (a morning routine), but his was a little extreme. And, when we say a "little," we actually mean so much so that if we ever wrote a book, we should make sure to include a story about it. Umm, here it is.

Our father worked in the tool and die industry for forty years. He managed a team at an office that sold these tools to manufacturers around the country. Anyways, he was supposed to be to work at 8:00 every morning, so like any true Preparer, he arrived at 6:30 so as to get some work done prior to anyone else arriving in the office. And, before leaving the house, he'd go through a strict morning routine. Here's that story we referenced earlier in this paragraph about him essentially being the poster child for the Preparer CORE, which he (and we) didn't know existed at the time (because it didn't).

Before going to bed (at exactly 11:00 after watching the show *MASH* or the *Tonight Show with Johnny Carson*), he'd prepare for the next morning. Again, likely something we all do, to an extent. But, read on. His Preparer tendencies were on full display every night and throughout his morning routine, which we'll explain now.

Each morning, on the kitchen table were the following items, placed in exactly the same locations the night prior: coffee cup, juice cup, spoon, knife, a jar of peanut butter, one cereal bowl, a box of Life cereal, a stack of coins, one stick of Wrigleys spearmint gum, a shoe horn (I can see some of you younger folks Googling "shoe horn" right now), and his keys. Nothing more, nothing less. Ever.

After waking up at exactly 5:30 a.m., our father would come into the kitchen dressed for work in his suit and tie. He'd then walk over to the toaster, push down the two pieces of white bread placed in there the night before, pour a glass of orange juice, prepare a cup of black coffee, pour a bowl of Life cereal, get the toast that had just popped up, spread crunchy peanut butter and grape jelly onto his toast and eat his breakfast.

Done one day: no big deal. Done every weekday in this exact sequence for forty years: Preparer. Sidenote: ironic, is it not, that while he was eating his Life cereal, he was preparing us for it through his actions (and, preparing for life is one key component of being a Preparer as you'll read later in this chapter). And you thought he was just eating cereal.

At the very moment he was done, he'd leave the dishes on the table for my mother to clean up later (not saying it's right, just saying that's how it was in our house back in the day), place the stick of gum in his mouth, place the stack of coins in his pocket, use the shoe horn to put on his shoes, which were waiting for him lined up next to his chair (always the right foot first), pick up his car key (of which he had on the table with the ignition key lying separate from the other keys for efficiency) and stand up to leave the house. As he took the precisely four steps it took to get from the kitchen table to the garage door, he would also bend down to grab his briefcase that he had positioned perfectly, with the handle already in the upright position next to the door, to leave the house for work (at exactly 6:00 a.m.).

He'd chew that single piece of gum on his drive to work, always arriving first, always parking in the same exact parking spot (backing into the best in the lot to ensure a smooth departure at precisely 4:30 p.m.). As for that stack of coins (you know you were wondering about them), he'd use those to buy two cups of coffee in the morning from the breakroom at the office. While we don't know for sure if he bought those coffees at exactly the same time each morning, I think that based on what we've learned about our dad, we actually can have confidence that we do.

Again, our dad may not have been doing this intentionally, but he was showing his sons how to be prepared for life by being organized, timely, responsible, consistent, precise, and more. He prepared us for life more than we're certain he ever realized.

## PREPARER DEFINED

Preparers "connect learning to life in a way that gets students ready for their future." At first glance, this may seem to be nearly the same as the definition of the Character-Builder CORE. Remember, Character-Builders, per our definition, *"move beyond academics to focus on the whole child and creating better people."* However, although there are similarities, there are definite differences.

We define **Preparers as those educators who want to create productive people, but more so from a workforce perspective.** They do so as far as focusing on what the person can do to help make the world a better place through their actions, including their choice of profession. They focus on ensuring that every student leaves with the skills and abilities to be a contributing member of society, in terms of the actual work they do to accomplish this.

Preparers know that our nation's future depends on a strong economy and that economy is fueled by people (our current students) ready to do their part in whatever job they're committed to doing. Again, Preparers want to grow a quality individual just like Character-Builders, but more so to result in quality employees (which is one of the major components of this chapter).

> Being a teacher, not only affects kids and learning, but it also affects our country's future and the future of the world. (James, fourth grade teacher)

After reading this chapter, you'll see how the Preparer and Character-Builder share many main beliefs, but ultimately, you'll recognize the differences that define them. And, who knows, we may have a few readers that previously identified as Character-Builders that switch over to connecting more with the Preparer CORE.

We believe that the CORE of the Preparer can best be further defined by breaking our definition down into three main subcategories. They are:

- Academics
- Employment
- Life

As you read this chapter, think about how, as an educator, all of your colleagues prepare students for future academic, employment, and life success. It's obviously a natural part of our jobs, regardless of your role. However, think about those colleagues who this seems to come more naturally to.

In the past, perhaps you thought they were overly focused on preparing kids for employment for example (obviously likely more evident at the high school level), when they should have been more focused on "getting through" the curriculum. Take their perspective for a moment. Consider that, though in this example obviously the curriculum is important, perhaps they see the bigger picture of preparing students to eventually be impactful in the work world, and strategically choose to make that a focus of their instruction in addition to the required curriculum. Maybe you could spend more time thinking about how the standards you are required to teach help prepare kids for the workforce, or how you could make it so.

## ACADEMICS

Purpose. A student's school experience during their childhood provides the foundation for a successful adulthood. If you're an educator who doesn't believe that . . . spoiler alert, you're in the wrong profession! **The most**

**effective Preparers engage students with their ability to connect the learning each day to a purpose**. And, not a purpose for learning that is defined by the adult, but rather the conclusion that students come to, conscious or not, on their own.

We mention "conscious or not," because we don't feel that all students, based on multiple factors, are able to recognize or articulate why they are captivated by certain teachers, lessons, or tasks. **Preparers successfully answer the age-old student question, "*Why do we need to learn this?*"** In other words, through their preparation, they ensure that the purpose of any activity is clear. Isn't this the ultimate goal of any teacher? To attain and maintain a position where students fully trust their instruction as being purposeful in their lives? Wow.

The same can be said for other roles in education. As a principal, are you clear about the purpose of tasks that you ask of teachers, assistants and other staff? As a district office person, are you clear about the purpose of tasks of those you supervise? If you're doing it right, you're avoiding the "*Why do we have to learn/do this?*" question in the first place. And, you certainly want to avoid your staff asking one another that at the water fountain.

Preparation. Preparers take their responsibility of creating young people who will be fully prepared for their future very seriously. So, what are those academic skills that are necessary to provide the capacity for success in the future? And ultimately, how do students then gain the ability to understand how mastering these connect to their probability of success, fulfillment, and happiness in the future? Let's dig into this further.

First of all, as we discuss these foundational pieces, we realize that we are not offering any groundbreaking information when we write about the numerous skills that educators introduce and instill in kids every day. That being said, we think that sometimes educators are too close to the work to recognize some of the most powerful things they do, or could do, for our students.

It's in the first grader who is learning how to share and to communicate their feelings. It's in the fourth grader who learns how to effectively work in a small group. It's in the middle school student who learns how to be proud of being their true self regardless of what others might say. It's in the high schooler who grows up to be confident in their abilities.

These are HUGE milestones for our students that we sometimes take for granted. And, are there curricular standards for any of these? Some, perhaps. In a way, they're bigger than the curriculum (and dare we say just as, or even more, important?). The truth is, for teachers, sometimes the busyness of the daily "grind" of teaching all of the required lessons (as well as everything else we do) causes many to unintentionally lose sight of why we are teaching the lesson in the first place, and/or how the curricular content could be connected to other important skills necessary for kids to be successful.

If you're a teacher, do yourself a favor tomorrow and consider that very topic for every lesson you teach. Then, communicate it to your students.

The more we consider the specific skills that we teach kids every day, the more it is apparent that there is not so much of a developmental timeline to follow, but rather that they are all skills taught in some way, at every age or grade level. These are basic, foundational skills like communication, collaboration, acceptance, conflict resolution, kindness, time management, organization and work ethic. As educators, we need to teach kids these things, and others, as soon as possible and then allow them to be practiced over the many years of their schooling and life. Are you doing this? In what ways?

It's interesting how, when you consider the same list of these foundational skills as it relates to young children with adults, their level of importance doesn't change over time. This is how you know that these truly are some of the foundational skills needed to prepare children to become successful adults.

Kids and adults need to be able to effectively communicate and collaborate with others. They need to be able to accept others, resolve disagreements, and simply be kind to one another (sidenote: kindness was suggested by one of our own children as a main thing that he learned in fourth grade this year). As a parent, how would you feel if your own child said that one of the main things they learned in a particular grade or class was how to be kind to others? Yes, I felt great too!

So, while we all agree that a big component of our jobs as educators is to prepare students through our academic instruction to be successful in life, for some of us it might be hard to see how we can do so given the required curriculum or other requirements of our job. After all, *"How do we fit it all in?"* Knowing that, we wanted to provide you with a few examples of how to incorporate the foundational skills that we have been discussing into the formal curriculum if you're a teacher. If you're not a teacher, no problem. As you read, reflect on how you can make your work in the lunchroom, at recess, or in your office have more of an impact on kids' readiness for the world.

As a first grade teacher, I'd like to share a few examples of things that I do with my students that are outside of (but connected to) the required curriculum. I believe they are examples of helping to prepare the students for the real world, even beyond the "academic" curriculum. As you read through them, think about the many great "life lessons" that you add to your instruction that also accomplish this same goal for the students you serve.

- *Writing—Partner/group writing:* On occasion I have students work together to write a story, taking turns writing the sentences and talking about their story along the way. These collaborative conversations, with necessary teamwork to reach a goal of a final written story, are skills they'll need in the workforce. What if you modified this idea for your own classroom tomorrow?

- *Reading—Show them what I'm reading at home:* It's not only important to *tell* kids about how important reading is (at any level), but it's also important to *show* them. I read a fair amount at night, and will every so often bring in my current read (I'm a first grade teacher, so kids are amazed that my books no longer have pictures—umm, errrr, at least too many pictures!) to show the kids the books they too could be reading when they are older if they keep practicing. Since not all kids have parents who show them how reading and learning is a lifelong skill that continues to be developed even into adulthood, it's important that I do. Could you do this, too?
- *Math—Communicate the Why:* For many lessons, I'll share with the kids at the beginning of the lesson why this learning is important for their future. Or, sometimes they'll brainstorm some ideas. We'll try to connect the lesson to how they might need this particular skill for a job, for a project around their house, and so on. Remember "Begin with the end in mind" (and communicate the end to your students . . . more on this later). How about doing this tomorrow?
- *Technology—Google document use:* I have students create a Google document with a question on it and "share" it with me. I then answer it and ask other questions as the conversation continues. No, not rocket science, but not part of the first grade curriculum either. These early technology-related skills and learning to clearly communicate via the computer are certainly going to be useful for them later in the world of work. What could you do to tweak this idea for your students?

Again, these are simply examples from one classroom. You've got your own examples in your own role. The point is, while much of this isn't in the curriculum, it is what the kids tell their parents at night when asked, "*What did you do at school today?*"

Educator: Review a recent lesson. Does it contain components that prepare students for their future? Or, does it at least include why the learning is important? If not, what slight modifications could you make?

Leader: When evaluating staff, do you regularly focus on how the teaching and learning prepares students for their future?

As we dive further into the foundational skills that students need to gain in order to be successful in the workforce, we'd like to offer another skill that is somewhat newer onto the educational scene. That skill is creativity. We're not suggesting that the skill of creativity is "new." Rather, that in terms of the centuries that we've been teaching kids, it's not until relatively recently that the power of leveraging student creativity to have a strong impact on academic learning has taken hold.

Today's educators are realizing the powerful (and sometimes uncomfortable) space that creativity has in the classroom. Treffinger writes, "We must empower students to become creative thinkers, critical thinkers, and problem solvers—people who are continually learning and who can apply their new knowledge to complex, novel, open-ended challenges" (2008). We believe that **creative thinking opens the door to critical thinking, problem-solving, innovation, and risk-taking.**

So, moving forward, when you think about preparing kids academically, please continue to do the good work you've always done. However, in addition, please consider (even more) the necessity to build in skills like communication, collaboration, acceptance, conflict resolution, kindness, time management, organization, work ethic, and creativity into your work. As you've learned, these may be even more important than the required components of your job, including the curriculum (but don't tell the curriculum director in your district that!). Said another way: Which skill have you used more recently, collaboration or conjugating a verb? Exactly.

## EMPLOYMENT

As we mentioned at the beginning of this chapter, Preparers create successful workers. We use "workers" here in a very general sense. Think of it as the actual act of doing meaningful work, not a job title or career choice. It's all-encompassing to include people's role in being in the workforce in some way.

Many schools have ways to connect life and employment skills that students are learning to the world of work. High schools, for example, often have work experience or co-op programs that allow students to put their learning into action.

Another great way to introduce students of any age or grade level to the skills that they'll need while working is a service learning experience. Service learning combines learning objectives with community service. **Service learning is a great first step to getting students *out* of the classroom and *into* practicing skills in real-life situations.** These situations are the same ones that they may encounter in the work world years down the road. Rifkin supports this when he wrote, "this will require significant shifts in approaches to teaching and learning, including efforts to integrate civic values into the school process. We need to expand opportunities for students to become more involved in their communities and make service learning an integral part of the academic experience" (1997).

Stop here and reflect on what service learning opportunities your students have (or don't have). Do you have that same feeling you had a few minutes ago when asked about the frequency your students need the skill of collaboration versus conjugating a verb? Exactly, again. It's ok, there's a first grade teacher out there right now, who happens to be the coauthor, who is brainstorming what else he could be doing with his students with regard to service learning . . . .

We think it is easiest for people to grasp the concept of service learning when using community service to help define it. **Service learning is community service, with a learning purpose**. Community service is helpful with learning in multiple ways. First, it is active, and many students find learning easier and more fun with activity. Second, it is interactive. It by nature demands that people communicate and collaborate with one another. Third, it yields a high level of engagement because it connects learning to real-life application. While involved in service learning, students often feel like they are having fun, not even recognizing that they're engaged in meaningful learning and work. More importantly, it's these experiences that will prepare kids for successful employment years down the road.

| Educator: Review your plans for an upcoming lesson or unit and add a service learning experience that aligns with the educational goals. Will it feel like a little "extra" work? Yes. It will also be what your students tell their parents about that night. |
| Leader: Challenge staff to have their class participate in a service learning experience and then support them in making it happen. Ask staff to document their activity and post pictures. |

I've shared multiple stories of entering my first administrative leadership position as an alternative education high school principal. Some of those stories involve practices that were in place long before I arrived. This is one of them.

I entered the principal position in 2013 and was introduced to a service learning and leadership class that was offered at my current school. Notice I said "class," not "club" or "after school activity." Coming from a social work background where I was committed to serving the needs of others, I was excited and intrigued to learn more.

Students were selected and invited to participate in the class based on their capacity or potential to collaborate, communicate, and lead. The class spent the first part of the year getting to know each other and building trust. Then, they brainstormed, researched, and planned community service projects. This is where I witnessed some pretty powerful moments.

The service learning experiences brought so many students "out of their shell." I would walk into that classroom or go to where a community service event was taking place and would be simply amazed. Students who I had witnessed as quiet earlier in the year or in other settings were having engaging conversations with other students and people they just met. They were obviously finding meaning in their service work. Basically, they were exhibiting the skills that we want to see not only in our students, but as adults in the workforce.

Community service events were typically ongoing, more than one-time occurrences in this class. They included things like visits to a senior living community, civic group meetings, quarterly blood drives, setting up events at our local library, working with the city's business improvement district, running holiday events for a group home for residents with disabilities, and much more. The power in these experiences was that students drove what and how they accomplished their tasks.

These experiences were powerful and definitely taught needed skills, but what's the overall purpose? **We believe that while the Preparer may appear to others to be teaching general life skills with little intentionality, they are in reality actually planning specifically to provide their students with experiences to ready them for future employment.** Service learning classes or projects are the perfect example.

The best service learning experiences are based on state standards, learning objectives and sound instructional planning and delivery. I hope this story about some powerful service learning experiences at one high school in Wisconsin specific to their impact on preparing kids for future employment propels you to think about how you can do the same for the students you serve.

Preparers plan with the end in mind. In support of that, "To begin with the end in mind means to start with a clear understanding of your destination. It means to know where you're going so that you better understand where you are now and so that the steps you take are always in the right direction" (Covey, 1989). Educators strong in the Preparer CORE take Covey's message very seriously. Their "direction" is helping kids be ready for their futures. Their "destination" is future employment for those very kids.

Even more so than service learning, an impactful way to encourage students to reach their full potential is to offer authentic learning experiences. Authentic learning is applying knowledge in real-life contexts and situations. One important note is that our definition goes beyond "authentic learning experiences" that are provided in the classroom. Rather, it describes authentic learning experiences as ones outside of the classroom in the "real world" doing "real-world" things (beyond even service learning as described previously). Read on if you're feeling a little foggy right now on the difference between "service learning" and "authentic learning experiences."

We'll clear it up in a minute by providing some examples of the latter. In the meantime, *What better way to prepare students for the real world of work than by involving them in a real-world task?* We need to be clear that this does not mean *mimicking* a real-world task. It's actually working to complete a task for and with a community or business partner.

In her online article called "5 Insights to Help Prepare Students for the Future of Work," Molnar writes, "The best way to help students acquire the skills they will need in the workplace is with 'active learning,' in which students are engaged in activities like reading, writing, discussion or problem-solving. This is followed by project-based learning and 'cognitive activation,' in which students are encouraged to focus on *how* they reached an answer, rather than the solution itself." Discussion, problem-solving, focusing on how they reached an answer . . . pretty important in the workforce, right? Here's how it connects to authentic learning experiences.

Let's lift the fog. Authentic learning takes service learning to a whole new level. Service learning, remember, is "community service, with a learning purpose." It can get students to take their learning outside of the school building, but it can sometimes lack the reciprocal relationship that authentic learning can accomplish.

The next level that authentic learning accomplishes, when done right, is a true partnership with a community organization or business. And when we say "partnership," we mean that it is a relationship that is mutually beneficial for both parties.

Molnar writes about students being engaged in real-world, problem-solving experiences. If these are truly "authentic" experiences, then by definition they have to be real. So, having students create an idea for their own business and then develop a way to market it (flyer, podcast, television commercial, website, etc.) is fine, but it's not real.

Real would be partnering with a business in town that can include your students with a real task or problem that they need solved. Often the best authentic tasks start out as problems. Maybe the business is slowing in sales and profitability and they need the class to investigate why and create a promotional plan to increase business. As you can see, this is beyond students providing a service, and is instead mutually beneficial for both the students and the business.

Guided by an actual employee of the business, students can participate in numerous tasks that have real-world implications. How powerful is that? And, many businesses will jump at the chance to partner with a school in their community. Partnerships like these are wins for everyone involved and in addition to a resolution to a problem can lead to things like positive press, employment opportunities for students, future funding sources, additional learning experiences, and more. Essentially, preparing kids for life. We'll share a story about that in our next section. Speaking of that, here's our section about how the Preparer prepares students for life.

## LIFE

Why does nearly everyone know the board game "Life"? You think it's because it was likely created around the time when you were a kid since you played it, but the truth is it was originally made in 1860. So, ummm, unless you're over 160 years old, you're wrong. To answer the question, we're all quite interested in taking the right steps to win in the "game of life" like we are in the game of "Life." See what we did there? We want to have the right job, buy a house, make decent money (love those Life "Paydays"!), get married, raise a few pink or blue children, and so on. It's, well, life!

At the end of the day, regardless of if you have "Preparer" in your CORE or not, regardless of your role, regardless of . . . well, anything, all educators want the students they work so hard for is to be successful in life. After all, the authors' definition of Preparer centers around preparing our students for whatever life has to offer them.

In no way does this minimize the importance of teaching academics, readying students for employment (or the million other things that educators do). However, when it comes right down to it, our most important work is in creating kids that will make a great life for themselves, making this world a better place today than it was when they found it, and as such making life better for those around them.

Warning: this subsection is going to read as quite simple, but that's intentional. When it comes to life, **Preparers help others find their purpose.** Finding purpose in life, while potentially a journey that can take a lifetime, is a topic we'll cover briefly in the next few paragraphs. There is that word again . . . *"purpose."* We started the book with this as a major focus. As you recall, we asked, *"What is your purpose for being an educator? What is your Calling or Reason in Education?"* It's been woven in throughout the book, and so it only seems fitting to wrap up the book the same way.

We believe that those educators strongest in the Preparer CORE may make the biggest impact on people. Stop and consider that for a minute, relative to your colleagues. You know that colleague who seems to be less focused than you are on teaching the curriculum or preparing students for the next grade. They may do more "projects" in their classroom that involve skills like collaboration, communication, and teamwork. Realize that their focus is more on preparing students to be successful in life through teaching these skills in addition to the curriculum.

We're not suggesting that they're right and you're not (or vice versa), we're just asking that you pause and consider this. You're both making a significant impact on your students. The truth is, they're lucky to have you both. Have you considered that perspective?

Whoops . . . there's another focus of this book coming back around again: *"**perspective**."* Perspective, of course, is the ability to see and understand the viewpoints of others. People in life who can understand the viewpoints of others are typically happier and more fulfilled in their work. In this book, we refer to it as the "unifying power of perspective-taking" because we know that a school staff with this ability to take others' perspectives have individual staff members who are happier and as such bring more happiness to those around them. And happy staff can accomplish anything.

We'd like to offer one final story, taken directly from the project-based high school that I work at now. While reading, consider the impact that these students had on their life during their school and well beyond as they participated in these experiences. Additionally, think about the words "purpose" and "perspective" from the lens of students and staff. Finally, ponder what makes this an "authentic learning experience" as opposed to "service learning." Here goes.

Since we know that as educators we are preparing students for life, we approached a senior living community near our school and asked for a meeting. As the meeting began, I got the impression that the director thought we were there to set up community service opportunities with them. After all, it is pretty common to have schools contact them to develop one-time community service experiences for their students.

Several minutes into the meeting, my colleague and I had to interrupt them and explain that we were actually looking for ways to have a true partnership, one where we could both equally benefit from one another. And, more specifically, one where we as a school would be trusted to work with them to help improve their business.

This clarification took us to a whole new level in our conversation. And the one question that shifted it all was, *"What's a problem that you are experiencing with your business?"* The initial answer had to do with the need they had which was regarding improving their website and finding ways to promote their business through social media. Um, did I mention that our school is filled with high school kids, whose phones are essentially glued to their hands at all times, often on social media?

So, we moved away from their initial thought of us coming over once to call bingo with the residents. Instead, we began working collaboratively with the marketing department to find ways to update their website and introduce other social media outlets into their business plan.

While in the end that was a success, it was only the beginning. I had no idea then and still to this day am shocked at how many additional ways our students would later partner with the senior living center. Here are a few things it turned into.

It turned into training and hiring students to work in food service. It turned into shadowing opportunities with nurses for students interested in the medical field. It turned into us having students work with the facilities department on the grounds. It turned into students developing a plan to assist new and current residents in learning and using email, the internet, social media, and so on. It turned into having a student learn the responsibilities of the front desk so the receptionist could take a lunch break every day. And, overall perhaps the best part is that oftentimes students came up with the solutions, ones that benefited both parties.

They were given the real-world problems within this specific business, they met with the employees who represented the departments in which the problems were occurring, and they came up with plans to resolve the issues. Real-world problems were investigated, considered, planned for, and solved by real students. It doesn't get any more authentic than that. And, what an impact on the lives of the students, staff, and residents!

As we end this subsection about how the Preparer does just that for the students they serve in terms of their preparing them for their own lives, consider this famous quote by Abe Lincoln: "In the end, it's not the years in your life that count. It's the life in your years."

Now, we can't compete with Abe (or his hat or beard), but we can underscore what those educators strong in the Preparer CORE already know: That educating students is about educating them for a fulfilling life. And, for them to have a fulfilling life, they'll need to know more than about conjugating verbs (English teachers, sorry for the reminder).

| Educator: Instead of asking students "what" they want to be when they grow up, ask them *"WHO"* they want to be.
| Leader: Have staff engage in a similar question as above. Instead, however, ask educators what they are doing to prepare kids for life. Essentially, what are they doing in their classrooms or in their role to prepare kids to have an answer to that question above that would make us proud?

## SUMMARY

There's "preparation" in the "traditional" sense of the word, and then there's "PREPARERation" in the "we just made up a word" sense of the word. But, we do so for good reason. All educators "prepare" to some extent, regardless of their role. However, an educator with Preparer at their CORE does so with great intention each day, in planning both for each day (and week and month) and on the go throughout the day.

As our definition indicates, they prepare kids for academics, employment, and life. Academically, the most effective Preparers prepare kids by teaching them skills like collaboration, acceptance, conflict resolution, kindness, time management, and organization. In addition to helping students out academically as they progress in their schooling, these skills will of course also help them beyond academics.

As far as employment, as discussed in this chapter, things like service learning and providing authentic learning experiences are key. It's through providing these types of learning experiences that students ready themselves for future employment.

Lastly, Preparers get students ready for life by understanding the power that they hold in the present to teach our students skills such as being caring, respectful, patient, and kind. See, your parents were right when you were a kid and they told you to "treat others how you would like to be treated." Preparers want kids to not only survive in life, but to thrive in it. So, get your PREPARATION CORE on today!

### Perspective-Taking Scenario

At your grade-level or department team meetings, you have a colleague who is constantly asking some version of, *"How does this learning connect to students' 'real lives'?"* She appears to be overly focused on this, instead of ensuring that the kids participate in the required curriculum to prepare them for the next class.

She's kind of a broken record. She talks a lot about this. It's kind of annoying. And, yet, at other meetings about things like reviewing test data or curricular topics, she doesn't speak unless spoken to. She seems disengaged. Why at some meetings is she so vocal and opinionated, and at others you barely even know she's there? And, a less obvious question: How can you leverage her strength in the area of preparing students for life (especially if that's not a particular strength of yours)?

## CORE Questions to Consider

1. How important is it to connect your lessons (or however you serve kids) to life outside of school? On a scale of 1–10, how effective are you at doing so? What could you do tomorrow to increase that number?
2. Consider your work for students. Reflect on what of it impacts their future, and what doesn't. For what doesn't, what's reasonable/possible to stop doing, or do less of, so that you can make more time to do more of what does impact their future (academic, employment or life)?
3. If getting students ready for real life is so important, as those strong in the Preparer CORE would submit, how come so many schools are slow to offer classes on things like personal finance, basic living skills, and/ or employability skills? Or, how come we often wait until high school to do so?

## We Dare You Challenge

Take one day, make it tomorrow. For every subject you teach, every period of your day, every group of students that you see, lead with how whatever they're doing that day will prepare them for their future. At the end of the day, reflect. Then, see where it goes the following day!

## Now What?/Action Steps

If this is your CORE, you should use it for the following actions:

- Care more about making better people and future workers, than better test-takers
- Successfully answer students' questions of *"Why do we have to learn this?"*
- Use your real-world experiences to influence kids
- Focus on the preparation of students for success in their future profession

Why Every Team Needs Someone with the Preparer CORE

- To keep staff focused on preparing students to be successful in the workforce

- To remind colleagues that what we do now has long-lasting effects
- To lead with "the why" whenever possible as an effective modeling practice
- To connect school data with how that correlates to real-world needs

How Identifying People with the Preparer CORE Helps My School Leader

- Keeps the leader grounded in what's important in educating kids
- Helps see beyond student achievement test score data
- Advocates for service learning in the school and community
- Ensures that community businesses are continuously provided high-quality applicants

How Understanding the Preparer CORE Helps Me Understand My Colleagues

- Those who disagree with the required curriculum may actually see its lack of connection to real life
- They realize that what's more important than drilling home content knowledge is preparing students to be positive members of society
- We're not just a school community, we serve the greater community outside the walls of our brick and mortar building
- "Preparing" students means so much more than preparing them to do well on the next big test

## Part III

# YOU ATE TO THE APPLE CORE

## NOW WHAT?

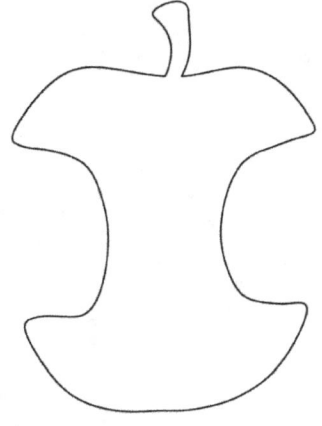

## Chapter 12

# Time for Apple Pie

*The future depends on what you do today.*

—*Gandhi*

"Time for Apple Pie." And, who doesn't like apple pie? Most books you've read take this final chapter to summarize everything you've already read once in the book. Since this book isn't like most, we'll skip the review and give you the (gentle) kick in the pants that you need to get moving, improving your service for students right now. The apple "APPLeY IT" graphic should be a strong clue.

We started this chapter with a Gandhi quote quite intentionally, for two reasons. First, it's hard to argue with a man whose first name, Mahatma, means "Great Soul." We, the authors, looked up what "Gary" and "Greg" meant (using a very reputable source—the internet). Let's just say that neither "Great" nor "Soul" came up.

The second reason we chose the Gandhi quote, and perhaps slightly more important, is because of his ACTIONS to fight against oppression, to peacefully protest against discrimination, and his introduction to the world of nonviolent methods such as civil disobedience. Yeah, there's that. His actions CHANGED the world forever. As an educator, yours can too.

Connected to this book: What's the point of reading this, or any, book? The answer is quite simple: to take ACTION to make a positive CHANGE. Specific to you as an educator, this can start tomorrow. No, wait, it doesn't have to wait that long. It can start tonight. No, wait, this just in, it can start NOW.

In the beginning of this book we challenged you to reflect on your current state as an educator. Today, is it everything you thought it would be when you signed up years ago? Likely, the answer is some version of "No." Regardless, the question after reading this book is, *"What are you going to do about it, right now?"*

In this book you learned about the ten COREs (Calling Or Reasons in Education). While we'll keep our promise of not reviewing them in this concluding chapter, we want to show you the graphic again for good reason.

| COREs | |
|---|---|
| Advocate | Connector |
| Changer | Energizer |
| Character-Builder | Helper |
| Collaborator | Innovator |
| Leader | Preparer |

Ultimately, this book was about two things: Purpose and Perspective. Meaning: reclaiming and fully utilizing your own purpose in order to feel fulfilled . . . and . . . understanding and trusting the perspectives of those you work with to achieve school goals. How does taking a quick look at the COREs above and reflecting on our definitions of purpose and perspective right now inform your next steps? Which COREs do you most connect with?

**Questions to Consider**

1. *Right now, in this very moment, are you fully utilizing your **purpose** for being an educator?*
2. Which COREs do you think the colleagues you're closest to connect with? *Right now, in this very moment, do you really understand and fully trust the **perspectives** of your colleagues (especially when they're different from your own)?*

If you're being honest, the answer to the two italicized questions isn't completely "*Yes*" to one or both of those questions. Perhaps, for one or both, it's even leaning more toward "No," and that's ok.

So, now what? We've focused this book on practical application for educators, giving you specific examples of things you could do differently for kids right away as a result of reading it. So, thinking about purpose and perspective, now seems like an opportune time to give you an additional suggestion for each, to do just that (kind of like the "APPLeY It!" sections you've read throughout the chapters):

**Purpose:** We've asked you this before: *Why did you choose education in the first place?* So, what's something you used to do years ago that aligned with your purpose that you no longer do? Likely, you don't "have time" anymore because of "everything else" that you have on your plate. While there's truth to that, there's still 24/7/365, last we checked, to do something about it. Get back after it.

Ummmm, what are you waiting for?

**Perspective:** Consider one major disconnect you are having with a colleague. (Insert pause here, for you to actually do it........) Now, put yourself in their shoes. Consider their perspective. Consider that they truely believe that their perspective is actually "right," not yours. Understand that you feel the same way from your perspective. Newsflash: You're not "right." Newsflash #2 (Somewhat less painful): They're not "right" either. Realize that it's just a difference in perspective. It's all good. Perhaps it's time you took the high road and tell your colleague this realization right now.

Ummmm, what are you waiting for?

There you have it. However, those actions are not the end. In fact, they're more like the beginning. You have other ideas in your head, other actions you know you must take after reading this book. While you've hopefully been taking written or mental notes along the way, we'd like to offer you another final opportunity now. These actions are the ones that will help get you back to the you that you knew when you started this gig years ago. Take some time now, and use the space below, to jot down a few specific actions to get you back on track:

_____

_____

_____

*The superior man acts before he speaks, and afterwards speaks according to his action.*

—Confucius

As much as it's hard to argue with the "Great Soul" Gandhi, it's also hard to argue with Confucius. After all, his name in part means "Master." While we're far from Masters (or Great Souls either), we believe our journeys as educators have led us to take action to write this book for you (and to get back at Jeff).

We're hopeful and confident in you, our fellow educators, to now use what you've learned to take action. You possess an amazing amount of power to change the lives of the students who you work with, either through your direct interaction with them or through the influence that you have on those who do.

We offer you a sincere "Thank you" for all that you do every day, for reading our book, and for the actions you'll take to improve your service for kids as a result. They deserve it.

# Bibliography

Anrig, Greg. "How We Know Collaboration Works," *Educational Leadership Magazine*, February 2015, 32.

Benson, Jeffrey. *Ten Steps to Managing Change in Schools: How Do We Take Initiatives from Goals to Actions?* Alexandria, VA: Association for Supervision and Curriculum Development, 2015.

Breaux, Annette and Whitaker, Todd. *Seven Simple Secrets-What the Best Teachers Know and Do*. Larchmont, NY: Eye on Education, Inc., 2006.

Buckingham, Marcus and Clifton, Donald. *NOW, Discover Your Strengths*. New York: The Free Press, 2001.

Burgess, Dave. *Teach Like a Pirate*. San Diego, CA: Dave Burgess Consulting, Inc., 2012.

Comer, James. "What Relationships Do for Learning" Blog Post, Connections-Based Learning Blog, July 2015, http://seanrtech.blogspot.com/2015/07/what-relationships-do-for-learning.html.

Cook, Lynne and Friend, Marilyn. *Interactions: Collaboration Skills for School Professionals-Eighth Edition*. New York: Pearson, 2017.

Couros, George. *The Innovator's Mindset*. San Diego, CA: Dave Burgess Consulting, Inc., 2015.

Covey, Stephen. *The 7 Habits of Highly Effective People*. New York: The Free Press, 1989.

Dweck, Carol. *Mindset*. New York: Ballantine Books, 2006.

Fisher, Douglas, Frey, Nancy and Smith, Dominique. *Better Than Carrots or Sticks: Restorative Practices for Positive Classroom Management*. Alexandria, VA: Association for Supervision and Curriculum Development, 2015.

Fullan, Michael. *Change Leader*. San Francisco, CA: John Wiley & Sons, Inc., 2011.

Gruenert, Steve and Whitaker, Todd. *School Culture Rewired*. Alexandria, VA: Association for Supervision and Curriculum Development, 2015.

Hierck, Tom and Williams, Kenneth. *Starting a Movement: Building Culture From the Inside Out in Professional Learning Communities*. Bloomington, IN: Solution Tree Press, 2015.

Hoerr, Thomas. *Fostering Grit—How Do I Prepare My Students for the Real World?* Alexandria, VA: Association for Supervision and Curriculum Development, 2013.

Johnson, Lisa. *Cultivating Communication in the Classroom—Future Ready Skills for Secondary Students.* Thousand Oaks, CA: Corwin, 2017.

Keith, Kent. *The Case for Servant Leadership.* New Jersey: The Greenleaf Center, 2015.

Lovejoy, Shawn. *Be Mean About the Vision: Preserving and Protecting What Matters.* Nashville, TN: HarperCollins Christian Publishing, 2016.

Marzano, Robert, McNulty, Brian and Waters, Timothy. *School Leadership that Works.* Alexandria, VA: Association for Supervision and Curriculum Development, 2005.

Maxwell, John. *Failing Forward.* New York: HarperCollins Leadership Publications, 2000.

Molnar, Michele. "5 Insights to Help Prepare Students for the Future of Work," *EdWeek Market Brief Magazine*, February 2018, 2.

Ridnouer, Katy. *Everyday Engagement: Making Students and Parents Your Partners in Learning.* Alexandria, VA: Association for Supervision and Curriculum Development, 2011.

Rifkin, Jeremy, "Preparing Students for 'The End of Work,'" *Education Update Magazine*, February 1997, 14.

Saenz, Adam, "Relational Readiness: The Four Must-Have Skills to Build Meaningful Relationships," *Association of Wisconsin School Administrators Magazine*, Spring 2017.

Schroeder, Joe. *Labor of Love: A Spiritual Companion for Servant Leaders.* Madison, WI: Self-published, 2017.

Taylor, Carolyn Stanford. "The Wisconsin Department of Public Instruction." What is the Educator Effectiveness System? Website: https://dpi.wi.gov/ee.

Treffinger, Donald. "Preparing Creative and Critical Thinkers," *Education Update Magazine*, Summer 2008, 26.

Warren, Rick. *The Purpose Driven Life.* Grand Rapids, MI: Zondervan, 2002.

Wikipedia. "Wikipedia: The Free Encyclopedia." Bridge. https://en.wikipedia.org/wiki/Bridge.

# About the Authors

**Gary Goelz** is an educator whose ongoing journey toward his CORE has offered him many different roles in schools. In his over twenty years of experience, he has been a kindergarten teacher, a first grade teacher, a building assistant (think assistant principal without the pay increase), a principal, a principal again, an assistant superintendent, and is currently a first grade teacher (again). His extensive writing background includes emailing, repeatedly teaching his first grade writers that "was" is not spelled "w-u-z," responding to even more emails, and making grocery lists. When not writing, Gary (who is widely known as the wiser, better-looking twin) enjoys spending time with his lovely teacher wife and their three daughters, who are still young enough to think he's pretty cool . . . as far as he knows.

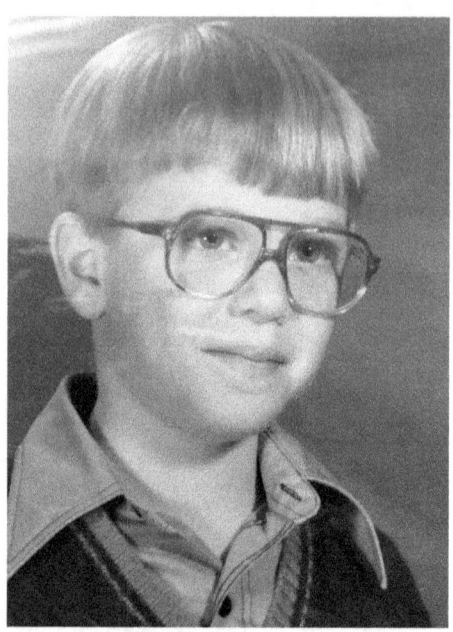

**Greg Goelz** is on a never-ending quest to humanize education. It's at his CORE. Years of experience in the fields of social work and school counseling have helped develop his collaborative, guide from the side leadership style as principal of an innovative and progressive project-based learning high school outside of Milwaukee, Wisconsin. In Greg's nontraditional education world, staff have the autonomy to do as they please and students are empowered to own their learning by being makers, not memorizers. He knows he is winning as a school leader when he is in charge of absolutely nothing. When Greg is not at school busy being in charge of nothing, he is at home doing much of the same with his SSW wife and three delightful (most of the time) children.

www.ingramcontent.com/pod-product-compliance
Lightning Source LLC
Chambersburg PA
CBHW051810230426
43672CB00012B/2684